DIECAST CARS
of the 1960s

Mac Ragan

Foreword by Ken Gross
Director, Petersen Automotive Museum

MBI Publishing Company

First published in 2000 by MBI Publishing Company, 729 Prospect Avenue, PO Box 1, Osceola, WI 54020-0001 USA

MBI Publishing Company books are also available at discounts in bulk quantity for industrial or sales-promotional use. For details write to Special Sales Manager at Motorbooks International Wholesalers & Distributors, 729 Prospect Avenue, PO Box 1, Osceola, WI 54020-0001 USA.

Library of Congress Cataloging-in-Publication Data
Ragan, Mac.
    Diecast cars of the 1960s / Mac Ragan
      p. cm. — (enthusiast color series)
    Includes index.
    ISBN 0-7603-0719-9 (pbk : alk. paper)
      1. Automobiles—Models—Collectors and collecting.
I. Title. II. Series.

TL237.2.R34.2000
629.22'12'075—dc21   99-087345

On the front cover: Toy cars of the 1960s were more than just playthings, they were beautifully crafted miniature examples of the real cars and trucks we saw on the road every day. As children, we took our toy cars for granted. Today, adults clamber to assemble collections of these diecasts, not only for their scarcity, but also for the memories they embody of care-free days spent driving the toys down the imaginary roads of our youth.

On the frontispiece: Toy cars, whether valued for their rarity or simply as a reminder of our childhood, are treasures that can turn up anywhere. Priced at not much more than it did when first released in 1969, this forty-cent Husky Willys Jeep turned up in a Cardiff, Wales, antique toy shop.

On the title page: The Volkswagen Beetle is recognizable to children, as well as adults, worldwide, making it more than an icon,. This happy little bug, made by Husky, first reached children's play roads in 1968.

On the back cover: Playing with ith a toy car, you always took the checkered flag, caught the bad guy, and moved loads that would have been insurmountable in the full-size counterpart. Toy cars were all this and more to us. It's no wonder that this photo of a Mini Dinky Jaguar XKE can send us back to those wonderful, fantastic car games of our childhood.

Edited by John Adams-Graf
Designed by Eric Aurand

Printed in China

CONTENTS

FOREWORD

Before any of us could actually drive, we had toy cars and trucks to satisfy that innate craving for wheels and motion. In the 1930s and 1940s, big Buddy L's, motorized spindizzies, smaller cast-iron playthings, and wood and balsa models were the rage—if you could afford them in tough Depression-era times. I grew up a bit later in the 1950s, and fondly remember having several metal dealer promotional models; a tinplate ride-em fire truck, a Schuco wind-up roadster, and lots of hard rubber cars. They were subject to every situation my friends and our little imaginations could devise...and in the process, they were battered, abused, and loved.

A few years later for most kids, British-built Dinkys and American Tootsietoys were the rage. Tiny, realistic, available cheaply, and in a great variety—every kid could have a fleet of them, and many did. Hours were spent fantasizing with these little replicas. We gave no thought to collectability. We traded, demo-derbied, modified and lost these cars with abandon. In truth, many of us longed for full-sized bicycles, then Whizzers and Mustang scooters...and finally real cars. But along the way, those virtually indestructable little die-cast cars filled a big void while we daydreamed, hung around at wrecking yards and gas stations, pored over car magazines and pestered older kids for rides. We couldn't own the real thing but those realistic, affordable little die-cast models made it possible to pretend.

Twenty years later, when my children were growing up, I hadn't had the foresight to keep any of my childhood toy cars, so they dove headlong into contemporary toys: Matchbox, Budgie, and Husky model cars, exactly the subject of this remarkable compendium by Mac Ragan. As a parent, I recall tripping over stacks of Mattel Hot Wheels and Matchbox cars of every description and short-lived Topper Johnny Lightning racers. Sadly, when their years of hard service were over and my kids grew too old to play with them, history was repeated. The cars were relegated, first to storage and ultimately to the trash....and along with them went memories of many happy childhood hours.

Today, every parent or kid who remembers the simple joys of die-cast toys will appreciate Mac Ragan's diligent work in compiling what will surely be acknowledged as the definitive study of these delightful toy cars and trucks. The terrific photography and illustrations will surely bring back fond recollections, and the detailed, carefully annotated text will assist any of you readers, who yearn for those bygone days to hit attics, old toy boxes, flea markets, and the Internet in search of the tough, little cars that so illuminated your past. And this time, paying much more for the models than you or your parents did a generation ago, you'll be more inclined to save those priceless boxes and blister packs.

Happy hunting... and to Mac Ragan, thanks for the memories!

Ken Gross
Director, Petersen Automotive Museum

INTRODUCTION

Toy cars of the 1960s were more than just playthings. They were not only beautifully crafted objects, but finely designed miniature examples of the real cars and trucks we saw on the road every day. As children, we took them for granted. They were cheap, plentiful, almost disposable. And we loved them. We imagined miniature construction sites, automobile dealerships, and table-top police chases. Most of us, usually with a friend, ran them into each other as hard as we could to simulate a real crash. As we grew older, we passed them on to a younger sibling or friend. Sometimes they were put away in a closet and forgotten—until, that is, our mothers told us they had been given away to some younger child who could enjoy them. Then, of course, we wanted them back, but it was too late.

This book examines just about every brand of small die-cast toy car made in the 1960s. Many names are recognizable: Matchbox, Husky, and Hot Wheels cars. Some are less familiar: Impy, Mini Dinky, and Siku, among them. If a child

The Commer "Walk-Thru" van was so-called because with both front doors open, it was possible to walk in one side and out the other. Introduced in 1965, this Husky truck sports two unusual features: a metal driver cast as part of the base and rubber suspension components.

played with toy cars, it was probably with these brands, the 45¢ dime-store cars that kids could buy with their allowance or money earned from mowing the lawn.

All the cars featured in this book are roughly 1/64th scale. More specifically, they are between 2 to 3 inches in length. Manufacturers weren't as concerned about the cars all being the same scale as they were with keeping their length under 3 inches so that a standardized size of packaging could be used. A good example is to compare any Matchbox car with a Matchbox bus. They're both about the same size, so it follows that the bus has been reduced in scale much more than the car—something probably close to 1/140th scale.

I want the photos I've shot for this book to take the readers back to a time when the biggest thing they had to worry about was washing their hands for dinner. I've chosen my favorite 1960s cars with the intention of showing them as we actually looked at them—the way children still examine their toy cars, up close, at eye level, imagining them as part of an exciting world of make-believe. In these photos, many of the cars appear to be the size of a real car. By featuring the vehicles this way, adults can more easily remember how they were seen by them as children. The scale I've chosen also reveals something that we may not have noticed: these toys were extremely accurate replicas of real vehicles of the day. And the cars of the 1960s were far from ordinary.

Penny, the 1/66th-scale line of toy vehicles from Politoys of Italy, produced this beautiful Alfa Romeo 2600 in 1967. Like all Pennys from the period, it featured full die-cast construction, save for the plastic windows, interior, and tires.

From the days when television only had three networks and milk was delivered door-to-door, Matchbox produced the Commer Milk Float (No. 21), mostly unchanged for seven years (1961 to 1967).

It is easy to say that the 1960s produced some of the most elegantly styled automobiles (rivaled only, perhaps, by selected models of the 1930s). The 1950s certainly saw a vast variety of wildly styled cars, but in the 1960s that flamboyance was tamed a bit. Cars were tailored, formalized, and flattened to a basic shape that lasted for 30 years. Only in the 1990s did the science of aerodynamics substantially change the look of automobiles. Gone are the crisp, knife-edged bodies of 1960s cars in favor of the rounded, lozenge-shaped silhouette of most cars today. Frankly, these later cars lack faces; they have little personality.

In the 1960s, car design was often about making a statement visually. Each year's style was different from the previous one. It was important to have the latest model—for reasons of status as well as aesthetics. Elegance was a recognized

commodity among the American people. Today, popular opinion has deemed a reverence for style old-fashioned and stuffy.

The photographs in this book are more than just documentary. Background colors were carefully selected to make each model stand out from the page or evoke a particular mood associated with that type of car. In these photos I seek to show the sophistication of 1960s automotive styling, a trait we seem to have lost during the last decade. Some photos show the entire vehicle; other shots reveal only a particular element which I believe exemplifies the appeal of that specific car. Many will recognize some of these toys and, perhaps, even remember driving the cars across the back of the living room sofa, or watching the tiny wheels bob up and down as they were run across gaps in the tiled kitchen floor.

CHAPTER 1

COLLECTING BASICS

For those with a preference for older cars and trucks, discontinued and "vintage" (generally considered to be more than 20 years old) toys can be enormously satisfying to collect. Obviously, these are more difficult to find. It's not possible to just walk into the closest Wal-Mart or other discount chain store and buy them. Also, older toys will cost more. Matchbox U.K. designer Martin Hickmore has this advice to collectors: "Get to know a good dealer or go to swap meets. If you can, go to swap meets in other countries to find variations you may have never seen." Most sources for vintage toys generally fall into six major categories: antique stores, mail-order, Internet, auctions, flea markets, and toy car swap meets.

Deciding What to Collect

Collecting toy cars like those featured in this book requires serious consideration of what to collect. That may seem obvious, but if the scope of the collection is not narrowed to a manageable degree, the collector can easily become defeated early on and give up the pursuit altogether. Since the 1960s, there have been scores of manufacturers producing an amazingly diverse array of toy vehicles. It is possible for anyone to have a first-rate group of cars in one or

For a young child, junkyards are a great source of fascination. Is it any wonder that a collector might want to make one in miniature? Even our most battered old toys can retain much of their original charm.

11

In 1965, Matchbox introduced its Trailer Caravan (No. 23) and, for the first time in one of their camping trailers, included an interior. In fact, the roof lifts off to better see the miniature built-in furniture.

two specific areas. Some people buy only one brand. Others choose a type of vehicle, such as fire trucks or grand prix race cars. Some decide on a particular manufacturer and collect a single make, perhaps Pontiacs. Still others focus on one decade, as this book does. It can be helpful to confine a collection to one scale, but if the focus is already limited (taxicabs or Maseratis, perhaps), it

makes sense to collect other sizes too. Most importantly, the collector should collect what he or she likes.

Prototypes, Preproduction Models, and Variations

A very specialized (and expensive) area of collecting is that of prototypes. These castings are made as samples for possible production,

BREAKING THE CODE

Like any specialized collecting field, there is a basic nomenclature among toy car specialists. The following grading terms and abbreviations are standardized references throughout the hobby.

Grading Terms and Numbers

MB or MIB . . . . .Mint in Box

MBP . . . . .Mint in Blister Pack

E . . . . .Excellent

NM . . . . .Near Mint

C10 or 10 . . . . .Condition 10, mint, never played with, may have a few small paint chips from packaging, shipment, or handling.

9 . . . . .Near mint, very minor play wear, a few small paint chips.

8 . . . . .Minor play wear with numerous small paint chips.

7 . . . . .Normal play wear with larger paint chips.

6 and below . . . . . . .Candidates for parts or major restoration.

Common Abbreviations

BW . . . . .Black wheels (Matchbox) or black walls (Hot Wheels)

BPT . . . . .Black plastic tires

brt . . . . .Bright

clr . . . . .Clear

drvr . . . . .Driver (referring to the plastic figure found in some cars, and often missing in older examples)

fl . . . . .Fluorescent (referring to the color of paint or plastic)

GPW . . . . .Gray plastic wheels

lt . . . . .Light (as in light blue)

met . . . . .Metallic (as in metallic green)

msg . . . . .Missing

orig . . . . .Original

RL . . . . .Redline (Hot Wheels)

RW . . . . .Regular Wheels (Matchbox)

SF . . . . .Superfast (Matchbox)

var . . . . .Variation

w/ . . . . .With

w/s . . . . .Windshield

WW . . . . .Whizzwheels (high-speed wheels used on Corgi Juniors beginning in the early 1970s)

Matchbox introduced the "near luxury" Opel Diplomat (No. 36) in 1966. As a toy, it remained popular in this country through the end of the decade—probably because it was the most "American"-looking foreign car in the lineup.

but end up never being issued. Preproduction models are used by manufacturers to test the dies (molds), paint and interior colors, wheels, and decoration variations before the toy is put into actual production. Ken Hill, design manager at Matchbox USA says, "If you want to buy prototypes, go to Hershey (an annual Matchbox convention and toy show held in Hershey, Pennsylvania) and buy them at auction. Usually dealers buy them to sell later, but anyone can purchase these if they're willing to outbid the dealers." Prices for preproduction models are very hard to establish since they are unique items. Roughly, they may sell at auction for $30 to $50. Prototypes bring much more, anywhere from $100 to $500. According to collector Charlie Mack, a few of these prototypes have been known to sell for over $1,000.

"It's easier to collect variations," Hill adds. A die-cast car is generally introduced in one color only, with no difference in decoration, interior color, or wheel type from car to car. Most castings will be recolored or changed at a later date to help freshen the line. This type of change is known as a variation, and today it is common for a model to go through several variations before the casting's life cycle is over. Collecting all of a manufacturer's current product line can be a challenge by itself, but looking for variations will add considerable intrigue to the search and keep collectors busy checking the latest stock at their local retailer.

The number of variations is much larger today than it was in the 1960s market. Mattel realized in the late 1960s that it was possible to wring more life out of a casting by changing its color scheme several times over the years. Most variations are produced in large quantities. The average "run" for a current Matchbox or Hot Wheels variation can be over 100,000.

Occasionally, a smaller quantity of a particular variation will occur. According to designer Ken Hill, "During the changeover process from one variation to another, mistakes can be made (wrong wheels, different interior color) that will cause a limited run of an 'unofficial' variation." There is much debate about how collectible these "mistakes" really are. The most prized variations are those that are planned, but for some reason the "run" is cut short and the numbers are limited to perhaps a few thousand copies.

Some mistakes may only affect a few models and those quantities are considered too small to qualify as a true variation. Consequently, these cars are only slightly more collectible than a standard model. Some such mistakes might include one make of car attached to a blister-pack marked with the name of another vehicle, contrasting styles of front and rear wheels, all four wheels being a different style from the standard model, and missing paint "decoration." Hill concedes that "You have

to go to the store often to find these limited-run variations." But we're doing that anyway, right?

Packaging

How important is it to keep a toy's original packaging? Among collectors, it is nearly unanimous that non-blister-pack packaging (i.e., a box) is a very important part of a complete collection. Even blister packs, such as those for early Corgi Juniors, can add substantial historical interest to a collection.

Just look at the box or package art from these older toys. In the 1960s most of the boxes or blister-pack cards featured a color illustration of the toy inside. As manufacturers pushed in the mid-1970s to keep retail prices down, the drawings started to disappear from the packages. Companies saved money because there were no artist fees, printing costs dropped since fewer ink colors were being used, and generic packaging meant lower overall launch costs. But remember, toy cars and trucks, not printed cardboard, are being collected. In other words, don't pass up a good model just because it's missing the box.

Major collectors generally agree that there is no point to saving the newer, generic packages, unless it's a Hot Wheels car where the current trend dictates that the toy be left unopened. For current varieties of Matchbox, or other brands, go ahead and open the package. Removing the car from a blister pack basically destroys the package (which is generic to begin with) so there is no reason to keep it. I usually cut (with a sharp box cutter) the clear plastic blister off, and save a few cards for future reference. Sometimes there is interesting information on the back—a listing of other models in the series, perhaps, or illustrations of play sets. If the

Matchbox's only American family sedan was a taxi! The Chevrolet Impala Taxi (No. 20) featured a driver and trailer hitch, presumably for those off-duty camping excursions.

package is unique for any reason to the car inside, save it; otherwise, dispense with it.

Grading methods

If a buyer cannot view a toy in person, he or she has to rely on some relatively subjective methods of evaluating its condition. The car and its package are graded separately, but both with the system described here. The best condition is "mint in box" or "mint in blister pack," abbreviated in print ads by most dealers as MB (or MIB) and MBP respectively. Some dealers go beyond that designation and list the condition of the car inside the box or blister pack. They generally use a 1–10 scale of grading, 10 being the best. This is very helpful because even new, packaged toys can be damaged or have slight imperfections from the factory. If a toy is listed as MB C10, it means that it is a factory-new (C10 means "condition 10") car still in its original box. Occasionally, a car will be listed as 10+. This means that the model is without defects, whether from the factory or otherwise. Condition 9+ can be quite acceptable, and generally indicates a toy with a very minor paint chip or a small factory paint blemish. Below level 9 the prices drop dramatically, but so does a model's condition. Stay away from these cars unless they can be restored without detection. I am not advocating restoring cars to then resell as mint. That is unfair to any future buyer. Restoration should only be done for the collector's enjoyment.

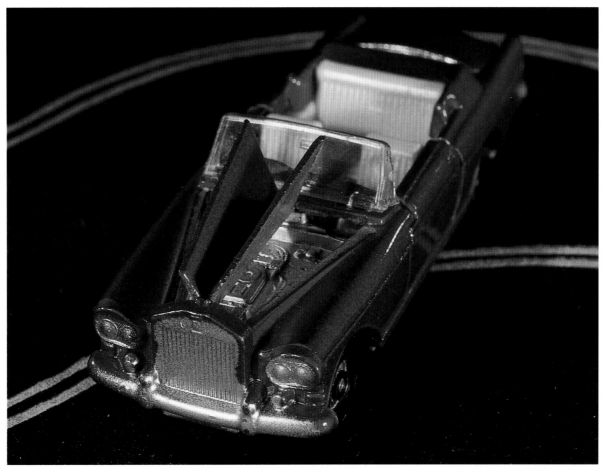

A rare feature in 1/64th-scale die-cast, this Rolls-Royce Silver Cloud's hood opens butterfly-style. The model's red color indicates that it's an Impy Flyer, a later series of Impy vehicles. Launched in 1968, Impy Flyers attempted to compete with Mattel's Hot Wheels cars by featuring low-friction speed wheels. Original Impy versions of this car were painted metallic silver.

CHAPTER 2

THE BIG FOUR: MATCHBOX, HUSKY, BUDGIE, AND HOT WHEELS CARS

The British deserve credit for creating the small, realistic, die-cast toy vehicles that were so popular in the 1960s. It was three such companies—Matchbox, Budgie, and Husky—that put these cars in just about every American toyshop, dime-store, and pharmacy.

The success of Matchbox in the early 1960s (by 1966 more than a million models had been sold) inspired other companies to create their own brands in an attempt get a piece of this rapidly growing market. The most successful of the early competitors was Husky, a line created by Britain's Corgi Toys in 1965 and marketed through the F. W. Woolworth dime-store chain. Hot Wheels cars, created by the American toy-giant Mattel, joined the market late in the decade. They had a profound effect on the industry because of their novel design and because of Mattel's aggressive marketing campaign. The competition included other British brands such as Impy, Mini Dinky,

Although Husky introduced this Buick Electra in 1964, a keen eye can discern that it's actually a 1959. (In 1960 Buick moved the license plate housing farther down into the bumper.) Husky used this casting for a police car as well, making for an unusually sporty and luxurious police cruiser.

19

Matchbox used its 1965 Ford Galaxie casting for a police car (No. 55) and a fire chief car (No. 59).

and Budgie, as well as non-British companies such as Majorette (France), Siku and Schuco (Germany), Penny and Mercury (Italy), Fun Ho! (New Zealand), and Johnny Lightning and Cigarbox (United States).

Matchbox

In 1947, Leslie Smith and Rodney Smith (no relation) created Lesney Products, Lesney being a combination of their first names. Lesney's first merchandise was not toys, but utilitarian die-cast products such as string cutters and ceiling hooks. Within a year, however, they made their first toy vehicles.

Several years later, in 1952, Lesney Products had great success with a die-cast model of the English royal coronation coach (complete with horses), ultimately selling over a million of them. That same year Jack Odell, a partner in the business since 1947, created a small matchbox-sized brass model of a

steam roller, put it in a tiny cardboard box, and gave it to his young daughter. The toy proved so popular with the girl and her friends that within a year, Lesney Products had designed and produced the first series of Matchbox toy vehicles. Part of the appeal, according to Lesney, was that children could now "buy a toy that was a complete toy for pennies." (In the United States the suggested retail price of a Matchbox car in 1960 was 49¢. The suggested retail price remained at 55¢ through 1969.)

Matchbox toys were made by Lesney at their plant in England, but were distributed by another company called Moko. Moko had exclusive rights to distribute Lesney Products in the United Kingdom, but Leslie Smith and Jack Odell (Rodney Smith left the company in 1951) had permission to sell their new series in other markets. In the late 1950s, Lesney struck a deal with New York toy distributor Fred Bronner, whose company, Fred

Considered the first "modern" Matchbox car because it featured window glazing, working suspension, and a separate plastic interior, the Jaguar XKE (No. 32) was introduced in 1962, a year after the real car debuted. Matchbox added delicately cast wire wheels and rich metallic burnt-orange paint to make it all the more spectacular.

In the 1960s, Matchbox made four versions of Volkswagen's legendary Microbus. The camper pictured here (No. 34) was introduced in 1968 and was the last of the series. Its short-raised center roof portion differs from the preceding model, which featured a higher roof with six windows.

Bronner Corporation, was granted the exclusive rights to sell the series in this country. That's why the Bronner name often appears on Matchbox pocket catalogues, carrying cases, and other related merchandise from the 1960s. In 1966, Bronner also launched the official Matchbox Collectors Club, where for one dollar a collector received a membership card, certificate, handbook, button, and a quarterly newsletter with the latest information about Matchbox and the activities of other collectors.

In the 1950s most Matchbox vehicles were replicas of British cars and trucks. The first American car, a Ford Customline Station Wagon, debuted in 1957. In 1960, a Ford Thunderbird and a Cadillac Sedan were added, and 1957's Ford Customline Station Wagon was replaced by a Ford Fairlane Wagon. The addition of American models picked up in the mid-1960s (Chevrolet Impala Taxi, Fire Pumper Truck, Ford GT-40, Studebaker Wagonaire, and Cadillac Ambulance) and by 1969 almost one-third of the series featured American vehicles.

By 1960, Matchbox had produced 75 different models. Through the decade, the policy remained that a model would be dropped only if immediately replaced by a new one, so that the total number of models in the series always remained at 75. This "1–75" series survived until 1999, whereupon Matchbox increased the number to 100.

In addition to the introduction of new models, the 1960s saw stylistic shifts in the way Matchbox cars looked. The most dramatic change was that new vehicles were being introduced with clear plastic windows. The first Matchbox car with windows appeared in 1957: the No. 33 Ford Zodiac Mark II. It was joined in 1958 by the No. 45 Vauxhall Victor. Soon thereafter, separate

Hot Wheels cars produced Dan Gurney's Indianapolis "Eagle" race car from 1969 to 1971. With Hot Wheels collecting intensifying in the past few years, this car remains a relative bargain with a market value near $50.

Matchbox's trend toward making more models of American vehicles continued with their Fire Pumper Truck (No. 29), issued in 1966. Many copies of this truck appeared with "Denver" decals on each door, just in case there was any question about the truck's origin.

The first concept-car model produced by Matchbox, this 1967 Lamborghini Marzal (No. 20) was introduced in 1969 as one of four all-new Matchbox vehicles to feature Superfast wheels. Unfortunately, the full-size version of this elegant four-seat luxury touring car never saw regular production.

MEET THE COLLECTOR
Charlie Mack

Charlie Mack, with five books to his credit (*The Encyclopedia of Matchbox Toys With Values, Lesney's Matchbox Toys, Regular Wheel Years 1947–1969*, among them), is America's most-published authority on the subject of Matchbox toys. Mr. Mack also founded the Matchbox USA club, maintains a Matchbox museum in his home, and organizes the annual national Matchbox convention, which he claims is the largest die-cast convention in America. He comments here on Matchbox toys.

Number of Cars in Collection

More than 22,000 Matchbox pieces. "I have one of every casting that Lesney and Matchbox ever made (except a very early and rare Lesney soapbox racer)."

Collecting Since 1967.

"It took me 10 years to get my first 1,000 cars. I was a kid in 1967, so naturally I played with my first cars. I did, however, try to keep them in good shape. Around 1969, I got serious about keeping them in mint condition. That's also when I joined the official (company-sanctioned) Matchbox Collectors Club."

Favorite Matchbox

"I can't name one specific car, but in general my favorites are the preproduction and prototype models. I bought many of these at auction, either at the annual Matchbox convention in Hershey, Pennsylvania, or at the convention I organize in Parsippany, New Jersey (the latter is the annual Matchbox USA Convention, held in June). I'm particularly proud of a group of 20 cars and trucks from the 1960s that were used for testing different paint colors."

The Packaging Issue

"The packaging is important if it has individual art on the boxes, as in the 1960s. But today there's no point in not opening a Matchbox blister pack unless you know the car is rare. Even then, if you like the cars out of the package, then take them out. The one exception is Hot Wheels. The market for them demands that they stay unopened."

Thoughts on the New, Limited-Edition Cars

"The Matchbox Premiere Collection cars may be a good investment. One thing I've noticed is that expensive 'collector'-quality vehicles do not sell well in the 2 1/2-inch size. It seems to work better in the 1/43rd and larger scales."

Favorite Collecting Story

"At a tag sale in 1990, I found a six-wheel crane (Matchbox No. 30B) in tan, not the usual silver. I paid $10 for it and in 1998 a collector offered me $5,000."

Advice to Collectors

"Start collecting the latest product line first, then work backwards. You'll be able to amass a sizable collection more quickly simply because the newer cars are more available. But most importantly, collect what you like."

Collecting Secrets

"At a toy show, if you see something you like, buy it right then because it may not be there when you return. Be wary of cars in extremely rare colors or with an unusual wheel variation. They may have been restored or altered."

Other Thoughts

"Use price guides, and if you're still unsure, contact an expert. I can be as thrilled finding a $1 car as much as finding a $1,000 car."

Husky introduced this Oldsmobile Starfire Coupe in 1966. It features an opening trunk and is one of the few full-size American cars modeled in Matchbox size.

plastic interiors and working suspension were introduced. The first model to feature all of these innovations was the No. 32 Jaguar XKE, introduced in 1962. I consider this car to be the first modern Matchbox; all future Matchbox vehicles would come to incorporate these design features.

Subtle changes were being made too. For example, the average length of the vehicles grew about half an inch, from 2 1/2 to 3 inches. Tires changed from metal or gray plastic to black plastic, and by the late 1960s, door, hood, and trunk lines became incised, rather than raised, for added realism.

By the middle of the 1960s, Matchbox cars were already collectibles. For example, the following text appeared in a 1966 pocket catalogue: "Some of the early models were perhaps simple compared with the super 'Matchboxes' of today, but even so they have now become collector's pieces and often change hands for much more than their original price."

By 1967, Matchbox's record sales earned it a place in the Guinness Book of World Records. But their dominance of the die-cast toy car market would soon end. When Mattel introduced Hot Wheels cars in 1968, sales of Matchbox products in the United States fell almost 80 percent. A year later, in an effort to compete with Mattel's cars, which sported dazzling paint colors, mag-style free-rolling wheels, and custom styling, Matchbox introduced their Superfast line.

At first, creating Superfast models involved fitting existing cars with free-rolling wheels and thinner axles. This entailed re-engineering the vehicles' base plates to accommodate the new axles. By 1971, Matchbox had replaced 20 models with new ones designed specifically for use with the Superfast wheels.

These included a more modern Volkswagen camper; a Dodge Charger Mk. III concept car (the second concept car produced by Matchbox, the first being the Lamborghini Marzal in 1969); a Rolls-Royce Convertible; and more bizarre designs such as the "Road Dragster," a fantasy vehicle with the engine occupying its entire midsection; the "Hot Rod Draguar," a wildly customized Jaguar XKE; and the "Rat Rod Dragster," a hot-rod version of the earlier, stock 1967 Mercury Cougar.

In its efforts to regain some of the market lost to Hot Wheels cars, Matchbox abandoned its legacy as a company that produced realistic toy cars to one that made hot rods and fantasy vehicles. Unfortunately, Mattel did it better with their Hot Wheels cars and, consequently, became the market leader.

Husky Models

Although Husky Toys were made for just six years and included only 66 models in its standard (2-inch) line, they were the largest competitor for Matchbox in the pre–Hot Wheels car era. Husky Toys were actually the product of the British toy manufacturer Mettoy Co. Ltd., a company that began producing a wide variety of tin, lithographed toys in 1933. But Mettoy is best known for its Corgi Toys, started in 1956 to compete with Dinky Toys.

Huskys might never have existed if the Woolworth chain of dime stores hadn't approached Mettoy in the early 1960s with an idea to produce a line of small die-cast vehicles to compete with Matchbox. Woolworth asked Mettoy to create a new brand name for the line. They wanted the vehicles to feature interiors, windows, and suspension systems just like the full-size Corgi Toys. In 1964, the Husky Toys brand was launched and became Woolworth's exclusive line of small, die-cast toy cars.

Because Husky Toys were designed to be sold in Woolworth stores in both the United Kingdom and the United States, the line included European and American vehicles. For instance, Husky produced British vehicles such as the Jaguar Mark X and XKE, Aston Martin DB6, Sunbeam Alpine, and Ford Thames Van. Notable American models included a 1959 Buick Electra, 1962 Ford

Husky's Bedford TK 7-Ton Lorry featured a die-cast "skip" and swinging support armature for loading and unloading. Commonly found with an orange body and silver-painted skip, earlier versions were painted maroon with an unpainted skip and armature.

Thunderbird, and 1965 Oldsmobile Starfire, the only models of these cars ever produced in this scale. These are, in fact, some of this author's favorite toy cars from the period.

As with Matchbox, the first Husky Toys were made in a slightly smaller size than later models. Several cars were replaced with larger castings of the same vehicle. Early Huskys were made with chrome-plated plastic base plates, while many later models featured metal base plates. Wheels changed too. The early wheels were made from a solid piece of gray plastic; later wheels featured black plastic tires mounted on either a metal or chrome-plated plastic hub.

The exclusive Husky contract with Woolworth expired in 1970. Mettoy decided that they could sell more of their toys by capitalizing on the Corgi name. Woolworth soon replaced Husky cars with the Playart Peelers line of die-cast vehicles while Mettoy

quickly changed the Husky name to Corgi Juniors. Old Husky models were relabeled with the new name, and development started on designs for new Corgi Juniors.

Budgie

Since their inception in 1959, Budgies have been thought of as a sort of poor man's Matchbox. Budgies were solid, simple models of mostly British cars and trucks. Made in England by Budgie Models Ltd., these toys were marketed until 1966 when the company went out of business. Another company, Modern Products, bought the rights to the Budgie name and continued production of Budgie models until 1969.

Throughout their 10-year history, Budgies were similar to early Matchbox cars in that they had no interiors, glass, or suspension (the only exceptions were the models of

Budgie produced this GMC Box Van dressed in Hertz Rental livery. It featured a metal swing-down door in the back.

27

28

convertibles, which included interiors and, sometimes, drivers). Despite these shortcomings, they were still popular toys in America and the line included models of cars not produced by other manufacturers, such as a 1967 Oldsmobile sedan and an early 1950s Packard convertible.

Hot Wheels Cars

With the introduction of Hot Wheels vehicles in 1968, speed and racing became the primary marketing agenda for die-cast toy cars. Until then, manufacturers created a broad range of vehicle types meant to be enjoyed by children when imagining real-life scenarios. Trucks were used in miniature construction sites, sports cars raced on makeshift road circuits, and ambulances and police cars rescued imaginary crash victims. Children used these toy cars to act out the plots they created.

The new trend focused on racing—but not racing on imaginary circuits built on Mom's kitchen floor. These new races were designed by Mattel to always take place on Hot Wheels track, strips of flexible orange plastic roadway that, combined with gravity, pulled their contestants to the finish line.

This trend lasted for almost 30 years. Consumers saw the effects of Mattel's speedy little racers on almost every other brand of 3-inch toy vehicle. Most manufacturers—from Matchbox and Corgi Juniors, to Cigarbox and Majorette—switched to low-friction "speed wheels" and started painting most of their cars in brilliant metallic and "custom" colors.

Hot Wheels cars sold in quantities beyond Mattel's greatest expectations: it was obvious that the public was ready for this

Hot Wheels cars marketed their "Gran Prix" series of racers from 1969 to 1971. The line included the Shelby Turbine, seen above, as well as a Brabham-Repco F1, Chaparral 2G, Ford Mark IV, Indy Eagle, and four others.

Mattel introduced Hot Wheels cars in 1968, and this 1967 Cadillac Eldorado was included in the "original 16" vehicles. Most models that year were mildly customized versions of everyday cars. Hood scoops, side pipes, and mag-style wheels were common features, even on such luxury cars as the Cadillac pictured here.

change to a racier image. The interest in speed and racing was perhaps inspired by the popularity of real "muscle cars" of the era, and the fact that organized drag racing was at its height in the late 1960s and early 1970s. With great success, the Hot Wheels line directly capitalized on the drag-racing frenzy by introducing, in 1970, models of the then famous Mongoose and Snake Funny cars that Mattel sponsored.

These, along with models of real grand prix and Indianapolis-style race cars, were perhaps the most realistic Hot Wheels vehicles made in the early years. The other models were either custom versions of late 1960s muscle cars, 1930s Fords (popular at the time with California hot-rodders), designs from famous 1960s car-cutomizers Ed Roth (the Beatnik Bandit) and Bill Cushenberry (Silhouette), "fantasy" cars created by Hot Wheels designers (Torero and TwinMill), or traditional models such as the Mercedes-Benz 280SL and Rolls-Royce Silver Shadow. Even these European luxury cars were fitted with red-line tires on mag-style wheels so that they could compete on Hot Wheels tracks. By 1998, Mattel created over 10,000 variations of Hot Wheels cars. The company claims that two Hot Wheels cars sell every second.

Hot Wheels vehicles didn't follow a numbering system like the one used by Matchbox, although they did introduce new models each year and phase out older ones with time. Mattel launched 16 Hot Wheels vehicles in 1968, and in a brilliant marketing move they offered each car in a variety of colors—at least 8, and sometimes as many as 14.

These early colors were called Spectraflame, in reference to the glimmering quality produced by their highly metallic, candy-coated look. Aqua, pink, magenta, and light green (sometimes referred to as "anti-freeze") were particularly striking. This was a complete shift from Matchbox, which used more realistic paint colors on its models and rarely changed them once a car was in production. The numerous paint color variations found with early Hot Wheels cars have added greatly to their collecting intrigue. Some colors were produced in smaller quantities and today command much higher prices. Pink, for instance, was unpopular with little boys who often shunned them. Finding a pink Hot Wheels car today is a challenge.

Hot Wheels cars were sold only in blister packs, which, when opened, were invariably thrown away. That's why today an early Hot Wheels car in its original blister pack will command many times the price of a Matchbox car from the same year.

Mattel also included a metal collector's button with each of the Hot Wheels cars made from 1968 to 1972. They were made to resemble a tire, the center section featuring an illustration of the car, and could be clipped to a shirt pocket. These buttons can still be found today, and add an interesting bit of history to any collection of early Hot Wheels cars.

The "California look" so associated with Hot Wheels cars went beyond the Spectraflame paint. Most of the vehicles had larger rear tires to simulate the characteristic "jacked-up in the back" hot-rod stance. The original "Custom" series cars (Barracuda, Camaro, and Cougar, among others) all had scoops on their hoods and exhaust pipes (except the Corvette) protruding from under the front fenders. Every car rode on mag-style wheels and red-line tires, a fad popular at the time with real cars. Most early models, although featuring opening hoods and detailed engines, lacked door and trunk lines, an omission that was not popular with collectors of more realistic-looking toy cars. That, however, made little difference to most children.

To make the new wheels roll more freely, the axles were made from very thin, flexible wire, ingeniously bent at right angles and tightly secured to the chassis to create a form of miniature torsion-bar suspension. The axle itself provided the "give"; installing an additional part to act as a spring (as in other toy cars) was not necessary. The wire axles, combined with speed wheels featuring a narrow edge to minimize contact with the racetrack's surface, really did make Hot Wheels vehicles the fastest toy cars available.

This speed, however, came with a price. The axles were so delicate that they easily bent out of alignment. Mattel quickly recognized the problem and offered a small metal "wrench" that was thin enough to fit between the wheel and the chassis—a tight fit, but the best angle for straightening the axle. The torsion-bar suspension was soon phased out in favor of a more durable design with straight axles made from stronger wire.

Mini Dinky

The detail, degree of accuracy, and often unique model choices made Mini Dinkys die-cast treasures of the 1960s. Meccano, British toy manufacturer and maker of full-size Dinky Toys since 1934, launched the Mini Dinky line in 1968 in response to the success of Matchbox toys. But Mini Dinkys were destined to fail because 1968 was also the year that Hot Wheels toy cars were introduced. The public now demanded toy cars that were speedier, racier, and more flamboyant in design.

The Mini Dinky line included models of American and European cars and trucks. The vehicles were designed under the "old order"—the pre–Hot Wheels era—and included such details as metal wheels with separate rubber tires, spring suspension, and functioning hoods and trunks on many vehicles. Each came packaged in a plastic box resembling a miniature garage.

Mini Dinky was the only company (with widespread U.S. distribution) to make 3-inch die-cast models of popular cars such as the MGB, the Cadillac Coupe de Ville, and a rather mundane American economy car, the Chevrolet Chevy II.

A word of caution to collectors. To reduce production costs, Mettoy produced the Mini-Dinky line in Hong Kong instead of England. As with other early die-cast models made in

A trio of Rolls-Royces. From left to right, a 1967 Silver Shadow, a 1969 Silver Shadow Convertible (both by Matchbox), and a 1964 Silver Cloud Convertible (Impy Flyer).

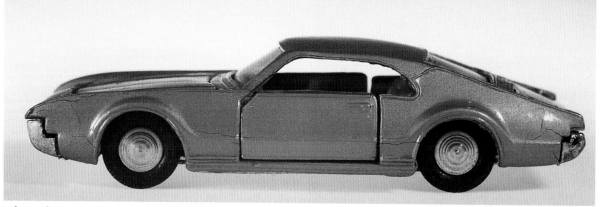

What a shame that this handsome 1966 Oldsmobile Toronado by Mini Dinky may eventually self-destruct due to metal fatigue. A common problem with Mini Dinkys, the condition is caused by an unstable mix of metals in the zinc alloy. Look closely to see that the paint has already formed a network of hairline cracks because of the metal's expansion underneath.

the Far East, large numbers of Mini Dinkys suffer from metal fatigue, which is caused by using a poor-quality alloy for die-cast parts. Look at a Mini Dinky very carefully before purchasing it. Sometimes they fall apart when handled, or have distorted sections of the body or chassis. Also, look for paint that has peeled or taken on an "alligator skin" pattern (a paint texture resembling reptile scales with bare metal showing in between). All of the above are signs of metal fatigue and it's best to avoid these models for obvious reasons. Still, it is possible to find perfect, or nearly perfect, examples today.

Impy

With the unwieldy name of "Lone Star Roadmaster Impy Super Cars," it's hard to know exactly what to call these die-cast gems of the 1960s. Since "Impy" appears larger than the other words on the packaging and advertisements, most often they are referred to by that name alone. Whatever we call them, Impys remain fine examples of die-cast toys, even surpassing Mini Dinky in quality.

The Lone Star Company of England started making toy cars in 1956. These first models were called Road-Masters (sic) and were slightly larger than Corgi Toys. By 1960, Lone

Impy's Merryweather fire engine measures almost 4 inches in length (not including the extended ladder). This imposing model features a die-cast body, chassis, and pivoting ladder platform. Notice the stabilizing jacks on either side of the rear wheel.

A trio of Impy Chrysler Imperial police cars. A Flyer version sits in the foreground, distinguished by its speed-type wheels, transparent blue (rather than opaque) emergency light, and red (rather than black) "Police" markings on the hood. It also lacks the rhinestone headlights of earlier Impy cars.

Star produced a line of highly realistic contemporary American cars, including a Chevrolet Corvair, Rambler Station Wagon, and a Cadillac Sedan. The name changed slightly to "Roadmasters" and the scale was reduced to match that of Corgi Toys. In 1966, the Roadmaster line was phased out in favor of the smaller Impy toys—almost certainly because of the success of Matchbox.

Impys had more special features than any other brand. Every car had functioning doors, hood, and trunk! In addition, all the cars sported jeweled (rhinestone) headlights, a feature found elsewhere only on some Siku and Penny vehicles of the period and on larger and more expensive toys such as those from Corgi. Impys also had working suspension and front wheels that "steered." Lone Star tried to include as many of the features of full-size die-cast cars (like Corgi and Dinky Toys) as possible. (Sometimes the opening features can actually detract from the overall look of an Impy car. The doors are the most common offenders, often misaligned when closed. Also, be certain that the rhinestone headlights are still in place.)

This 1963 Chrysler Imperial by Lone Star Impy of England, along with most other Impy cars, features an opening hood, trunk, and doors, as well as steerable front wheels and rhinestone headlights.

Siku produced this hefty model of a Ford F-500 truck in the early 1960s. Like other Sikus of the period, it features rhinestone headlights and a metal body and chassis. Of note are the red-painted undercarriage, double rear wheels, and suspension components made of rigid wire rods.

Impy was the only line to make a 3-inch Chrysler Imperial, Rolls-Royce Silver Cloud Convertible, and a Volvo P1800S. In 1968, like every other manufacturer of die-cast toy cars, they felt the pressure to switch to low-friction speed wheels to better compete with Hot Wheels cars. These new Impy models—mostly old castings but with speed wheels and fresh paint colors—were called Flyers. They lasted until the mid-1970s, and, with time, some of the appealing features (including working doors) for which Impys were known were discontinued.

Siku

Since the 1950s, the German toy maker Siku has consistently produced high-quality miniature cars and trucks. In 1963 they introduced their "Traffic" series of die-cast vehicles. These models, all numbered, include the letter "V" prefix, for *Verkehr* ("traffic" in German). Siku made scores of European models, with an emphasis, not surprisingly, on German vehicles. Especially popular

were Opel, Volkswagen, Mercedes-Benz, and European Fords.

Siku hasn't always had widespread distribution in the United States, even though from the beginning they made an effort to produce American cars such as the Oldsmobile Holiday Sedan and Buick Wildcat Coupe.

Sikus were made in a slightly larger scale (1/60th) than Matchbox vehicles (approximately 1/64th), which resulted in some American cars being over 3 inches in length. The proportions were sometimes exaggerated, making the sedans more elongated and flatter than the real cars they represented. Perhaps Siku's designers were influenced by the illustrations of real cars in American advertisements and sales brochures of the period, which often pictured the cars wider and lower than they really were. Print advertisements for early 1960s Wide-Track Pontiacs are good examples of this exaggerated depiction.

Other distinguishing features of Sikus include rhinestone or clear plastic headlights, detailed interiors, windows, and working suspension. Some had folding seatbacks and others featured plastic "drivers" behind the steering wheel. Most had moving parts, and if the trunk opened it often contained a spare tire. These kinds of details make Sikus unique and highly coveted today.

Majorette

Good distribution in the 1980s made Majorette vehicles almost as common as Matchbox cars in the collections of American children. But, sadly, the company has all but retreated from the U.S. market; their beautiful new models of such contemporary European vehicles as the Porsche 996, Mercedes-Benz CLK GTR and A-Class, Renault Kangoo van, BMW Z3 Coupe, Ford Ka, and the Audi TT are nearly impossible to find.

The French toy company Majorette started producing die-cast cars in the early 1960s, small numbers of which reached the U.S. market. The first models were mostly of French vehicles (Citroën, Peugeot, and Renault), with a few German and Italian cars added to the mix. Majorette was also known for producing a variety of trailers (horse, boat, camping, and others) for the cars, often packaging both together as a set. American cars joined the line in the 1970s, but throughout Majorette's history the emphasis has been on European marques.

The early cars are quite realistic, featuring opening parts, window glass, and plastic interiors. Proportions are generally correct, but the wheels on some models tend to be too small. Overall, though, the early Majorette vehicles are very appealing and add

Majorette packaged its Formula 3 race car with a Renault 16; today, the company still markets cars and trailers together in twin packs. The diminutive racer has a plastic chassis with a notch on the underside designed to slip over a raised mounting point on the trailer.

Tootsietoy's tiny earth scraper is the perfect size for moving miniature jellybeans. Unlike Mini Dinky's 4-inch Michigan Scraper, this earthmover is only 2-1/2 inches long and its body is molded as one piece, not two.

a great deal of interest to any collection of 1960s toy cars.

Tootsietoy

No book on die-cast toy cars of the 1960s would be complete without mentioning Tootsietoy, the American company that invented the die-cast toy car in the 1930s. By the early 1960s, their vehicles seemed a bit crude compared to Matchbox cars, which by then were featuring windows, interiors, suspension, and separate base plates. The small (3-inch and under) Tootsietoys didn't always include these features, but perhaps because they were less expensive than Matchbox toys and readily available, they were very popular with American children.

Other than the wheels and axles, most Tootsietoy models were made from a single piece of die-cast metal. Base plates were rarely used; the vehicle's axles were crimped to struts molded into the underside of the car's body. The result was a "hollow" body shell, open at the bottom, on most closed cars (cars with roofs). Convertibles included interiors molded as part of the body casting.

Examples of 1960s Tootsietoys are a Ford Falcon, Ford Sunliner convertible, Ford Ranch Wagon, Studebaker convertible, Rambler station wagon, Volkswagen Beetle, and an Indianapolis racer. Construction vehicles, also very popular, were often sold as sets of four or five trucks.

Cigarbox

Introduced in 1968 by Aurora, the plastic-model-kit and slot-car giant, Cigarbox Miniatures actually used the plastic bodies from the slot-car line. These bodies were attached to a die-cast metal chassis instead of the slot car's plastic chassis (which held the electric motor). Cigarbox cars also featured interiors, windows, aluminum wheels, rubber tires, and suspension. With a name clearly intended to remind the buyer of Matchbox toys, these cars came packaged in a miniature cigar box, something unimaginable in today's politically correct times.

Early Cigarbox models are more realistic-looking than later ones. After Mattel introduced Hot Wheels cars, the Cigarbox line was changed in an attempt to be more competitive. Aurora added the name Speedline. The plastic bodies became plated with chromelike metal, often tinted purple, pink, or gold. The wheels changed from the handsome aluminum and rubber design to a single plastic mag-wheel and tire combination. The design was proportionately too large for most of the models, giving them a more toylike appearance.

But in the pre–Hot Wheels car era, Cigarbox Miniatures could be quite realistic. The company also made models of cars not commonly found in the 3-inch size, including a 1967 Ford Galaxie XL-500 and a 1963 Buick Riviera.

Johnny Lightning

Johnny Lightning, made by the Topper Company from 1969 to 1971, shamelessly copied the Hot Wheels style. They made cars with wild, fantasy designs and fitted them with low-friction, mag-style wheels. They also sold tracks and accessories that were similar to Mattel's products. Johnny Lightning tried to gain exposure by sponsoring Al Unser in the 1970 Indianapolis 500 (he won the race). But that wasn't enough to keep Johnny Lightning in the die-cast car race, and Topper went out of business in 1971.

In their attempt to compete with Hot Wheels cars, Johnny Lightning models were almost entirely fantasy vehicles. The casting and paint quality were good, but unfortunately the wheels were poorly executed—proportionately too large with silver mag-wheel printing crudely applied. This design flaw, along with the decision to produce vehicles with no basis in reality, kept Johnny Lightning from ever becoming a serious threat to Mattel's Hot Wheels vehicles.

Johnny Lightning was reborn, though, in 1994 when the Playing Mantis Company

In an effort to compete with Hot Wheels vehicles, Cigarbox altered its original cars in the fall of 1968 to create the Speedline series. This 1967 Ford Galaxie XL-500 reveals the chromed body and one-piece mag-style wheels used on Speedlines. Earlier Cigarbox cars featured unpainted plastic bodies and handsome aluminum wheels with separate rubber tires.

Penny of Italy made this beautiful early 1960s Maserati 3500GT, the first car Maserati produced in any significant numbers. By concentrating on Italian vehicles—everything from Alfa Romeo and Fiat to Iso Rivolta and Ferrari—Penny made many models of cars not produced by other manufacturers. Their high level of detail and relative scarcity today make them pricey.

purchased the trademark and began launching several new series, including Muscle Cars USA, Mustang Classics, and Truckin' America. Unlike the Topper Johnny Lightnings, these new vehicles are realistic and of high quality.

Lindberg

In the late 1960s, Lindberg, the American plastic-model maker, introduced the "Mini-Lindy" line of plastic kits featuring Matchbox-sized cars and trucks. Although not die-cast metal, these kits did include four metal bars, which the builder could hide between the model's seats and chassis, giving it greater weight and making it seem more substantial when handled.

Exterior details on these vehicles were very good. Interiors, glass, and separate chrome-plated wheels with black plastic tires were typical features. It was also possible to find models that no other manufacturer made in this scale: an Austin-Healey 3000, 1968 Mustang Fastback, Willys Jeepster, and a GMC tow truck are just a few examples.

Penny

Penny, the 1/66th-scale line from Polistil, an Italian toy maker known primarily for their 1/43rd-scale die-cast cars, was introduced in 1966 and produced through the early 1970s. The Penny line reproduced all types of vehicles, including racing cars and trucks. The quality was good, with most cars featuring suspension, windows, and interiors. Don't look for any American makes, however. Almost all of the models are of Italian vehicles, such as Alfa Romeo, Fiat, Ferrari, and Lancia.

Mercury

Another Italian company, Mercury (which started producing die-cast toy cars in the 1940s and enjoys a reputation for quality on par with Corgi or Dinky Toys), introduced the "Speedy" line of 1/66th-scale cars in the 1960s. These cars, like Mercury's larger vehicles, featured opening parts, full interiors, and window glass. Speedys were not easy to find in the United States in the 1960s, although some were imported. A good source for these today are the Internet auction

Schuco, a revered name in the German toy industry, introduced a line ofs 1/64th-scale vehicles in 1969. Included was this Büssing Open Truck, here carrying dried black-eyed peas. Although this truck lacks an interior, Schuco cars did feature them. Overall, Schucos are some of the most handsome and realistic miniatures of the late 1960s, providing delicate casting details in a very small scale.

sites. Prices are slightly higher than for Matchbox cars of similar age.

Schuco

The famous German toy manufacturer Schuco introduced a line of 1/66th-scale diecast cars in 1969. They were beautifully crafted, with full interiors and glass, opening parts, and fine body castings that incorporated such delicate details as side window pillars and trim moldings—features that other manufacturers simply ignored. The vehicles that Schuco reproduced were almost exclusively of German marques such as Opel, Mercedes-Benz, Porsche, Volkswagen, and Audi. To Schuco's credit, they equipped their 1/66th-scale line with the most handsome low-friction wheels of any toy cars of the period: a two-piece design

(wheel and tire) that accurately simulated real wheels of the period. As realism was a Schuco hallmark, no mag-style wheels were ever used.

Fun Ho!

Fun Ho! was a line of die-cast vehicles made from the early 1960s to the middle of the 1970s by Underwood Engineering in New Zealand. They were not distributed widely in the United States, and consequently are extremely hard to find today. The quality was very good for the period, and the Fun Ho! line included models of Australian cars—vehicles not commonly produced by other toy manufacturers. Among them were several Holdens, an Australian Ford Falcon, and a simple, but accurate, open utility trailer designed to be pulled behind a car.

A Matchbox Pontiac grand prix (No. 22) pulls a load of star-shaped pasta in a tiny utility trailer from the New Zealand firm of Fun Ho! Like Matchbox cars from the early 1960s, Fun Ho! vehicles were small (only about 2 inches in length), and did not include interiors, window glazing, or suspension.

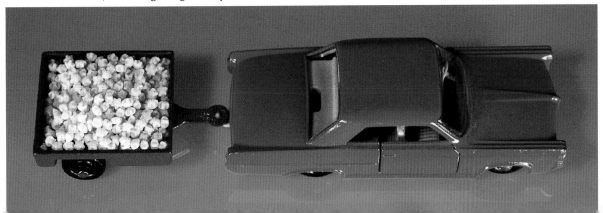

CHAPTER № 4

IT'S A MATTER OF TASTE:
Luxury and Personal Luxury Cars

Luxury Cars

We wished that our parents drove these cars. We saw the cars on television, on the street, in magazines, and sometimes in our neighbor's driveway. But most children's parents didn't drive Cadillacs, Imperials, and Lincolns, and especially not Mercedes-Benzs or Rolls-Royces.

In 1960s America, the size of the car was directly related to its place in the auto pecking order. Thus, luxury cars were larger than the average sedan. Ford, Chrysler, and General Motors would often stretch their "large car" chassis and use it as the basis for their "top-of-the-line" luxury vehicles. Sadly, miniatures of these American luxury cars are particularly scarce because most die-cast toy cars of the 1960s were designed and made in Europe, where big American sedans were rarely seen. Curiously, European luxury cars were reproduced only slightly more than their American counterparts. Toy designers must have been concentrating on what they thought kids wanted most: sports cars, emergency vehicles, and construction equipment.

If, as children, we were lucky enough to have a luxury car in our collection, we

One Matchbox Lincoln Continental (No. 31) overtakes another on this twisty stretch of miniature highway. The metallic blue car on the left was introduced in 1964; the bright mint-green example came later.

The Matchbox Rolls-Royce Silver Shadow (No. 24) was one of the most popular toy luxury cars of the 1960s. Introduced in 1967 (two years after the real car was launched), it featured an opening trunk and a rich metallic ruby-red paint not found on any other Matchbox vehicle of the era.

treated it with special care. We protected its smooth, painted finish, and didn't play with it outside in the dirt with our other vehicles. It was as if those little luxury cars were imbued with some of the same prestige of their full-size cousins.

We created miniature roads on the backs of upholstered sofas or made parking lots on top of broad, flat ottomans. We packed their miniature trunks with imaginary luggage, and sent them off, at a stately pace, on make-believe holidays. Upon arriving at our destinations of tiny restaurants or hotels, the cars drove up slowly and quietly, without screeching tires or other dramatics.

The two best-known luxury car miniatures were made by Matchbox: a 1964 Lincoln Continental (No. 31) and a 1965 Rolls-Royce Silver Shadow (No. 24). Who can forget that strange, bright, mint-green paint on the elegant Lincoln, or the beautiful, deep ruby-red metallic color of the Silver Shadow? Interestingly, both models had opening trunks, a feature perfectly suited for those imaginary picnics and trips to the country. As for the

strange color on the Lincoln, I can only imagine that it was an attempt to make the car look as little as possible like the black Lincoln Continental in which John F. Kennedy had ridden in Dallas. The Matchbox version, introduced in 1964, must have been in prototype stage in late 1963.

Matchbox also introduced the Jaguar Mark X (No. 28) in 1964. Since Jaguar was known for its performance-oriented cars, Matchbox designed this model so that its hood opened (realistically hinged at the front) to display an accurate die-cast version of the Jaguar's famous double-overhead cam (DOHC) 4.2-liter six. This was a popular model that stayed in the Matchbox line for four years. It was painted an actual automotive color—but just try to name that shade. In its day the color was called bronze; today some might call it metallic taupe.

In 1963, Matchbox introduced the Mercedes-Benz 220SE Coupe (No. 53), and it was followed in 1968 by the Mercedes-Benz 300SE Coupe (No. 46). Although in Europe these may have been considered upscale family cars, in America Mercedes-Benz was exotic enough in 1963 to be thought of as a luxury car.

In 1966 another "premium" European sedan entered the Matchbox line—the Opel Diplomat (No. 36). Painted metallic gold for its entire manufactured life, this popular model weathered the transition into the Superfast line. Wearing its original, pre-Superfast wheels, the Diplomat was a handsome car. It was one of the most "American"-looking European sedans, which probably explains its popularity in this country. The only clue that this car wasn't of American origin was its rectangular headlights, a feature that was not legal on real cars in our country until 1975.

The Marzal was a 1967 concept car from the three-year-old Italian exotic-car manufacturer Lamborghini. It was introduced to the Matchbox line in 1969 as model number 20. Although the real four-seat touring car was never for sale, it was reproduced by numerous toy companies, including Mercury, Penny, and Playart. (Playart's 1/64th-scale line, Peelers, replaced Husky Toys when the Husky contract with Woolworth ended in 1970.) The Matchbox version came in a rich metallic red and has the distinction of being Matchbox's first model of a concept car and one of the first four completely new models produced with Superfast wheels (the others being the No. 5 Lotus Europa, No. 56 BMC

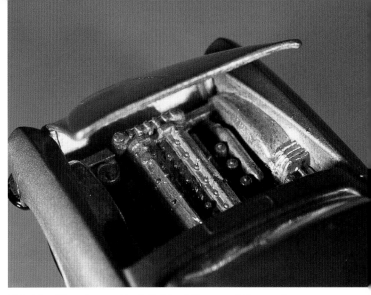

This Matchbox Jaguar Mark X (No. 28), one of the most popular models reproduced in miniature (Matchbox, Husky, Impy, and Fun Ho! all made at least one), featured an accurately cast example of the big Jag's double-overhead cam (DOHC) 4.2-liter six-cylinder engine.

1100 Pininfarina Sedan, and No. 69 Rolls-Royce Convertible).

Husky made a Buick Electra, a Jaguar XJ6, and, like Matchbox, a Jaguar Mark X. Hot Wheels cars, known for their racing and fantasy designs, only made one luxury car in the 1960s—the Rolls-Royce Silver Shadow. Mini Dinky also made only one—the Cadillac Coupe de Ville.

Impy had its version of the ubiquitous Jaguar Mark X, as well as a Mercedes-Benz

The modest—even elegant—fins of the 1964 Cadillac Coupe de Ville would disappear by the next model year. This Mini Dinky features an opening hood and trunk, and came packaged, like all Mini Dinkys, in its own miniature plastic garage.

Matchbox introduced its Mercury Cougar (No. 62) in 1968. It featured steerable wheels (operated by pressing down on either side of the car), opening doors, and a trailer hitch. Find one painted light yellow and it may be worth over $1,500 to some collectors.

220SE, a Rolls-Royce Silver Cloud Convertible, and an elegant light metallic blue 1963 Chrysler Imperial Coupe, complete with a correctly shaped, rectangular steering wheel.

Siku produced two Cadillac Fleetwoods and a Mercedes-Benz 600 Pullman (limousine). Budgie made an early 1950s Packard Convertible, their only luxury car. Although Tootsietoy made numerous Cadillacs, Lincolns, Chryslers, and Packards in their larger (6-inch) series, luxury cars were rare in the 3-inch and under range.

Schuco's precisely cast 1/66th-scale series was launched in 1969 with a Mercedes-Benz 200 and an Opel Admiral 2800E (both "near luxury" vehicles) in the assortment. Fun Ho! had its own version of the Jaguar Mark X, as well as a Rolls-Royce Phantom V and a Mercedes-Benz sedan.

Personal Luxury Cars

What is a "personal luxury" car? They always have two doors (that's the personal part) and feature a body style not shared with any other model in the company's lineup. Ironically, they do not have to be made by a luxury marque. The Ford Thunderbird is a good example. They are not, however, simply two-door versions of a four-door sibling. For example, a Cadillac Coupe de Ville is a two-door version of a Sedan de Ville, and therefore doesn't qualify for this category. The Cadillac Eldorado, with its unique body style is, however, part of the personal luxury group. Also included in this category are the great Grand Touring (GT) cars of Europe such as the Maserati Mistral, Jensen Interceptor, and Iso Grifo. Like other personal luxury cars, a GT's purpose was to transport occupants comfortably, quickly, and in style.

This category is rich with toy car examples, perhaps because it's closer to the popular sports car genre. Early models include Matchbox's Jaguar XK140 Coupe (No. 32), introduced in 1957, and the Aston Martin DB 2/4 (No. 53), introduced in 1958. Both cars were still in the Matchbox line in 1960. In fact, that year saw the introduction of Matchbox's 1958 Ford Thunderbird (No. 75). The real 1958 Thunderbird, with its bucket seats and center console, is often credited with creating the personal luxury niche. Two important personal luxury cars were added to the Matchbox line in 1968: an Italian exotic called the Iso Grifo (No. 14), and a first-generation Mercury Cougar (No. 62), the luxury version of Ford's Mustang.

Husky introduced its 1962 Thunderbird in pink; later versions were yellow and are fairly easy to find today. The company also made a 1967 Cadillac Eldorado. Only the

Bertone styling and a Corvette engine; no wonder they were so expensive. Matchbox introduced its Iso Grifo (No. 14) in 1968, converted it to a Superfast model the following year, and discontinued it in 1974, the same year that real Iso Grifo production ended. The sapphire-blue color of early models helped make this one of Matchbox's most popular and handsome cars.

bright blue version is a Husky; metallic green models, although made from the same molds, are Corgi Juniors from the early 1970s. Husky also produced an Aston Martin DB6 in metallic gold, purple, or green (silver was reserved for the James Bond version), and a Jaguar XKE 2+2 (in dark red metallic).

The Hot Wheels line included mildly customized versions of a 1967 Mercury Cougar, Cadillac Eldorado, and Ford Thunderbird, as well as a 1968 Lincoln Continental Mark III and a Maserati Mistral. Mini Dinky produced one of the all-time great personal luxury cars, the 1966 Oldsmobile Toronado, in factory-correct light metallic blue. Topper's Johnny Lightning line offered more wildly customized versions of the Cadillac Eldorado, Oldsmobile Toronado, and Ford Thunderbird.

Car connoisseurs will recognize this Husky as a model of the 1962 Ford Thunderbird. (The three decorative trim pieces on the rear fender tell all.) This yellow version was packaged with a transparent blue-tinted plastic hardtop (removed for photography) and was sold at Woolworth's from 1966 to 1968.

Originally presented as a styling study by Ghia, the 2300S became a regular production model for Fiat from 1961 to 1968. This Impy model accurately recreates the semifastback styling and reverse-slant C-pillars, which were typical of Ghia-designed coupes of the period.

Impy reproduced the sporty and elegant Fiat 2300S Coupe. The Impy Flyers line added a Maserati Mistral and a Cadillac Eldorado. Siku made a variety of personal luxury cars from around the world: an Oldsmobile Toronado, Maserati Mistral, Lincoln Continental Mark III, and a Lamborghini Espada among them.

Cigarbox is of special note because it was the only company that produced a Matchbox-sized 1963 Buick Riviera, the icon of "personal luxury" cars. Cigarbox also made a 1967 Ford Thunderbird Coupe and a first-generation Oldsmobile Toronado.

Penny produced a number of expertly crafted miniatures of Italian personal luxury cars. These included, among others, an Iso Rivolta, Lancia Flavia Zagato Coupe, and a Maserati 3500GT and Mistral. These were spectacular cars in real life, and Penny did an admirable job of capturing their fluid lines and elegant paint colors. They are real 1960s die-cast gems.

Following Spread:
Lone Star Impy's imposing Jaguar Mark X outsized and outfeatured the Matchbox version. Both cars featured an opening hood, but the Impy also included an opening trunk and doors, as well as steerable front wheels.

The exemplar of personal luxury cars, the 1963 Buick Riviera was rarely modeled in small-scale die-cast. This Cigarbox version features, as do all Cigarbox cars, a die-cast chassis mated to a plastic body. The spun aluminum wheels were some of the most handsome on any toy car of the period.

MEET THE COLLECTOR
Jim Gallegos

Jim Gallegos probably has the largest collection of toy cars in the United States. He considers himself a collector only, for he never sells any of the pieces or exhibits them to the public. Here are facts about his collection and some comments from him.

Number of Cars in Collection
25,000 Matchbox, 15,000 Hot Wheels, 8,000–10,000 Dinky, 8,000–10,000 Corgi, plus thousands more in other brands.

Collecting Since 1968.

Favorite Matchbox
1965 Ford GT (No. 41) and 1967 General Motors Greyhound bus (No. 66). "I still have the ones I played with as a child. In general, I prefer Matchbox regular wheels, early Yesteryear cars, and Major Packs."

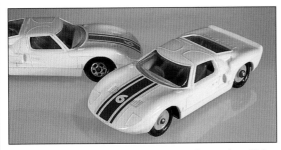

A favorite of prominent collector Jim Gallegos (he still has his original from childhood), Matchbox's Ford GT (No. 41) features a detailed die-cast V-8 engine visible through the rear window glass. An "original wheels" version is parked in the foreground; a Superfast models sits behind it. Notice how the wheels and the color of the racing stripe changed. Later Superfast versions are painted metallic bronze.

Changes Seen as Matchbox Moved From the 1950s to the 1960s
"Before the 1960s, Matchbox wasn't as consistent with the sizes of their vehicles. In the sixties, they became much more uniform. The 1960s also introduced interiors, glass, and other plastic parts."

The Packaging Issue
"The original box is a big part of the history. It adds much to the collection. If the car is blister-packed, generally it's okay to take it out of the package."

Thoughts on the New, Limited-Edition Cars
"In the 1950s and 1960s, as today, toy cars were meant to be enjoyed primarily by children. That's why it's harder today to find those toys in mint, original condition. New collectibles will be kept unopened, or at least mint, so the supply of good examples will always be high, preventing the values from rising over time."

Favorite Collecting Story
"I found a mint condition Matchbox Prime Mover (No. 15) yellow (an extremely rare color) at a toy show in 1985 for $40. Within 10 years its value increased to over $2,000."

Advice to Collectors
"Select one area to start collecting. For example, fire trucks, or the Matchbox 1–75 line. Most importantly, collect what you like. Do not buy for investment purposes; it's pure speculation as to what the market will do. The Hot Wheels craze of the late 1990s may fade in the years to come. Realize the limitations of your budget. Use the many reference books available and talk to experts to make sure you're buying from reputable dealers."

Collecting Secrets
"Ask train shop dealers if they have any loose Matchbox cars lying around. They often are included with old train collections the shop purchases."

Other Thoughts
"Remember that these toys were and are made for children. Many adults are taking this aspect away by competitively hoarding new models as they appear. Let your kids enjoy playing with these cars, just as you enjoyed them when you were a child."

CHAPTER № 5

THE NEED FOR SPEED:
Sports and Racing Cars

How many American children knew what a Lamborghini was until Matchbox produced their Miura P400 in 1969? How did we know what Ferraris looked like before Matchbox introduced their classic 250 Berlinetta in 1965? These were the toys that opened up the international world of automobiles to a generation of American children.

The toy sports cars of the 1960s ranged from the everyday Mustang and Camaro to such exotic foreign cars as Lotus, Ferrari, and Lamborghini. Together, Matchbox and Hot Wheels cars featured 15 different sports car models during the 1960s. Mini Dinky, even with its small group of vehicles, featured five sports cars: a Jaguar XKE, Chevrolet Corvette, Mercedes-Benz 230SL, MGB, and a Ford Mustang. In fact, at least seven companies made models of the Ford Mustang: Matchbox, Hot Wheels cars, Mini Dinky, Impy Flyers, Cigarbox, Lindberg, and Mercury. The Chevrolet Corvette was equally as popular. Hot Wheels cars, Mini Dinky, Impy, Impy Flyers, Siku, Cigarbox, and Lindberg all made models of the Sting Ray.

Sports car toys also endured some of the roughest play. It was these cars that most often, with the help of a childhood friend, were crashed head-on into each other

Penny of Italy included this Ferrari, and 13 additional Formula 1 cars in its lineup. All featured authentic racing colors, plastic drivers, simulated wire-spoke wheels, and unique bodies for each style of car.

In the late 1960s, the venerable American toy maker Marx Toys attempted to compete with Mattel's Hot Wheels cars with a line of small die-cast vehicles. Marketed as both Mini Marx Super Speed Cars and Blazers, the Hong Kong–made toys featured die-cast bodies and base plates, full interiors (often with drivers), and speed wheels mounted to the axles with a press-fit plastic bearing similar to those found on Hot Wheels vehicles. This Camaro features a beautiful candy-blue paint finish, and although its overall proportions are accurate, front-end details are crudely modeled.

One of the best-known sports car toy from the 1960s, the Matchbox Ferrari 250 Berlinetta (No. 75) was introduced in 1965. For several years it featured handsome wire wheels; in the late 1960s they were changed to a simple chromed disk style. Matchbox added Superfast wheels in 1970 and changed the paint color to bright red.

across kitchen floors. We also ran them side by side in imaginary rally races, popularized at the time by movies such as *The Love Bug* and *Munster Go Home*. Invariably, there would be a crash, and the resulting paint loss just added to its realism. Today, unfortunately, these badges of competition greatly lessen the value of the toys.

Some of the most realistic models of sports cars were made by Matchbox. The MGA (No.19) had been in the line since 1958 (it was preceded by an MGTD). In 1962, Matchbox introduced its spectacularly handsome Jaguar XKE (No. 32) and 1965 brought the famous green Ferrari Berlinetta (No. 75). Later models included accurate versions of a Mercedes-Benz 230SL, Ford Mustang Fastback, and Lotus Europa.

Oddly, Husky only made one true sports car: the Sunbeam Alpine. But what a good

Why aren't these people looking at their fabulous car? Arguably the most beautiful vehicle of the modern era, Mini Dinky faithfully reproduces the svelte lines of the Jaguar XKE in 1/65th scale. One can only hope that it doesn't begin to self-destruct from metal fatigue.

The brilliant metallic teal color and mag-style wheels of this Impy Flyer 1964 Corvette Sting Ray help make it considerably more striking than its original Impy cousin.

choice because no other manufacturer produced a model of this classic 1960s roadster. (Husky did make a Jaguar XKE 2+2.) Another sports car legend (and the author's first real car), the MGB, was made only by two companies: MiniDinky and Fun Ho!

The Mercedes 230/280SL series, however, was very popular in miniature. Matchbox, Mini Dinky, Siku, Penny, and even Hot Wheels cars had their own versions. Another popular sports car of the late 1960s was the Lotus Europa; Matchbox, Impy Flyers, and Mercury all made replicas.

Penny offered a fascinating assortment of finely executed Italian sports cars. Some of the more unusual and beautiful models include a Ferrari 250GT Lusso, Alfa Romeo 2600 Sprint Bertone, and Alfa Romeo Giulia SS.

Schuco introduced its 1/66th-scale line at the end of the decade with a large assortment of European vehicles. The BMW 2002, Ford Escort 1300GT, Porsche 911S, Opel GT, and Ford Capri 1700 are a few examples of these highly detailed replicas.

Racing Cars

Ironically, the manufacturers who sold the majority of die-cast models in the United States during the 1960s—Matchbox, Husky, Budgie, and Tootsietoy—actually made far fewer racing cars than some of their competitors. While Matchbox did make 5 open-wheeled (Indianapolis- or Formula 1–style) race cars, Penny of Italy made 14. Matchbox also made 3 close-wheeled (bodywork surrounding the wheels) racers, but Cigarbox made 12. Even more intriguing is that Husky made only one race car—a Ferrari Berlinetta—while Impy made none. And although drag racing had been popular in America for years, no miniature pro-stock vehicles,

James Bond's Aston Martin DB5 became the most famous car of the 1960s. So why did Husky use a DB6 body for its version of Mr. Bond's well-known Goldfinger-fighter? The working ejection seat helped most kids overlook this rather major error.

funny cars, or rail dragsters were made in the 1960s (the Mongoose and Snake funny cars entered the Hot Wheels line in 1970).

This burst of Formula 1 and grand prix car models came near the end of the decade, when the glamour of international grand prix races such as Nürburgring and Monaco was at its zenith, and when the Indianapolis 500 was one of the most-watched sports events on television.

The chance today of finding toy race cars remaining in mint condition is fairly low. These cars really saw rough play. Kids could watch the actual cars practically every weekend on ABC-TV's *Wide World of Sports*. Crashes were common (and replayed over and over), as the drivers of these expensive machines couldn't always control the tremendous power produced by their engines. Mimicking such scenes from television, toy racers were hurled down wood-floored hallways, across kitchen floors, and even down stair banisters. By design, Formula 1 cars had exposed wheels, and they were the first part to fly off in these simulated crashes. Sometimes the axles themselves bent (especially the wire type used by Hot Wheels cars). And finally, the miniature drivers found in many of the

With an uncharacteristically smooth paint finish, Tootsietoy's 1960s-style Indianapolis racer appears to have been dipped in dark green lacquer. These 2-inch cars were often sold in "Jam Pac" sets, appearing in stores well into the 1970s.

open Formula 1 cars would often be thrown from their vehicle upon impact, only to be lost and eventually swept up by the vacuum cleaner.

Before the introduction of Hot Wheels track, children invented their own race circuits on the floor or sometimes hand-drew them on big sheets of paper. The outcome of the race was decided by the "drivers." But to win a race on Hot Wheels track required the fastest car. Usually set up with two parallel tracks, (always running downhill, as gravity was the power source) a Hot Wheels heat was more like a drag race than a grand prix circuit full of turns. Speed and mechanical design became more important than a completely accurate appearance. It didn't matter so much if a toy car was realistic-looking, as long as it could beat another one on the track.

But before Hot Wheels cars arrived, Matchbox produced what became the most well-known die-cast racing car of the decade: the Ford GT (No. 41). This model

Matchbox introduced its Lotus Racer (No. 19) in 1966, a year after Jim Clark won the Indy 500 in a similar car. Other than the color, Matchbox's own BRM Racing Car (No. 52) appears to be a twin of the Lotus; closer inspection, though, reveals different bodies and engine castings.

Preceding Herbie in Walt Disney's *The Love Bug* by one year, Matchbox introduced its Volkswagen 1500 (No. 15) in 1968. It remains one of the most accurately proportioned models ever produced of the classic Volkswagen Bug. Dressed up with Monte Carlo Rally plates, the Beetle was painted off-white, then later, as a Superfast model, became metallic orange. Production ended in 1971.

preceded by one year the famed Mark II GTs that finished first and second at Le Mans in 1966, beating rival Ferrari for the first time. The Matchbox GT remained in the line until 1971. Usually painted white with a blue stripe running down the center of its hood, this model featured a detailed, die-cast V-8 engine visible through the rear window glass. The Ford GT (often called GT40) was also produced in miniature by Siku, Cigarbox, Mini-Lindy, Tootsietoy, and Mercury.

Also from Matchbox were two grand prix–style racers, a Lotus (No. 19) painted British racing green, and a BRM. (No. 52) in royal blue. Although introduced one year apart—1965 and 1966 respectively—they seemed designed as a pair, having similar proportions and identical wheels. Of special note from Matchbox was their off-white Volkswagen Beetle (No. 15), introduced in 1968. Modeled after the Monte Carlo rally version, this miniature remains one of the most accurate ever made of the classic Volkswagen Bug.

Hot Wheels cars excelled in producing miniature racing cars, and this Ford Mark IV is no exception. A soft light from above highlights the fluid lines of this powerful race car. The rear section flips open to reveal a detailed, diecast V-8 engine.

Hot Wheels cars offered a large selection of both closed- and open-wheeled racing cars. Their first true race car was part of the "original 16" introduced in 1968. It was the Ford "J," precursor to the Ford Mark IV, which won Le Mans in 1967. In 1969, Mattel introduced eight new racing cars—from the Indy-style Eagle and Shelby Turbine to Can Am's Chaparral 2G and McLaren M6A. All are accurate versions of famous racing cars that were not often made by other toy companies in this scale.

Of special note are the Italian manufacturers Penny and Mercury. Penny produced 15 different Formula 1 cars from teams such as Brabham, Eagle, BRM., McLaren, Ferrari, and Lotus. Mercury made six Formula 1 cars plus seven closed-wheel types such as the Porsche Carrera 6, Chaparral 2F, and Ferrari 250 "Le Mans."

And finally, Cigarbox made 12 accurate models of closed-wheel racers—everything from McLaren, Lola, and Cobra to Ford and Willys. The company also produced an assortment of Formula 1 cars.

MEET THE COLLECTOR
Everett Marshall

Everett Marshall is the founder of the Matchbox Collectors Club, owns and operates the Matchbox Road Museum in Newfield, New Jersey, and is one of the country's largest collectors of Matchbox products. Here are some of his thoughts on these toys.

Number of Cars in Collection
Over 17,000 Matchbox toys.

Collecting Since
1980. "It was that year when I was out shopping for toys with my three-year-old son and one store had all of their Matchbox toys on sale for half-price. I bought one of each [for himself!]."

Favorite Matchbox
"King Size models, especially the ones displaying real promotional advertising."

Changes Seen as Matchbox Moved From the 1950s to the 1960s
"The wheels changed from all metal to gray plastic, then to solid black plastic. Some models were made with black plastic tires mounted on chrome-plated plastic hubs. Also, in the 1960s Matchbox starting producing more models of American cars. Before that they were mostly British."

The Packaging Issue
"For cars of the 1960s, it's important to save the packaging. For toys generically blister-packed, it isn't. You can't properly display a car unless you take it out of the blister pack and there's no need to save the package once it's open."

Thoughts on the New, Limited-Edition Cars
"Only buy them if you like them. It's probably safer to stay with cars that Americans can relate to, like the Dodge Viper."

Favorite Collecting Story
"While visiting the English town of Enfield, which is near the old Matchbox factory, I went into a shop that sold closeout merchandise. This shop contained a closet filled entirely with King Size Matchbox cars and trucks, one of my favorite groups. I spied an Articulated Horse Box (Matchbox K-18), which was painted a color that I'd never seen before. I snapped it up quickly at a price that I'll simply describe as 'cheap.' The Horse Box was usually painted orange, but the one I found was tan, like the illustration in the Matchbox catalogue."

Advice to Collectors
"Decide what you like, whether it's cars, trucks, farm toys, or whatever. Start with current products, then work backwards. If you're collecting the Matchbox 1–100 line, try to find all of those from the current year, then start to fill in your collection from the previous year and so on.

"Make sure what you buy is really what the seller says it is. In 1998 I was offered a large group of Matchbox toys and was assured they were all in good condition. I looked at a few of the pieces—all were in excellent condition—so I bought the collection. Later, upon looking at each piece, I discovered that the cars I first saw were not representative of the rest of the batch.

"And finally, use the published price guides for rough estimates only. Contact an expert if it's an important piece or a collection."

Collecting Secrets
"Buy new castings as soon as they arrive in the stores. The quality will be best then because the dies are new. It's smartest to concentrate on new castings of contemporary cars."

CHAPTER № 6

GETTING THE JOB DONE:
Construction, Service, and Emergency Vehicles

Construction Vehicles

Construction equipment, reproduced more than any other type of 3-inch vehicle, includes the expected miniatures of dump trucks, bulldozers, cement mixers, cranes, and pickup trucks, as well as more specialized vehicles such as scrapers, graders, skip trucks, and Jeeps. (Delivery trucks, unless specific to construction, are discussed in the "Service Vehicles" section.)

The most-reproduced vehicle was the dump truck. Matchbox alone made nine versions from 1960 to 1969. Husky, Mini Dinky, Impy, and Budgie all made at least one dump truck of their own. Bulldozers and crane trucks came in a close second, with most models produced by Matchbox, Mini Dinky, Impy, and Budgie.

Unlike luxury and sports cars, construction vehicles saw a good deal of outdoor play. A typical site was often under an old tree where the grass was thinner and the dirt closer to the surface. Muddy hillsides were popular too, as well as the cool, flat dirt underneath a raised wooden deck or back-door stairs.

Wherever the location, we could be engrossed for hours—carving roads out of

A typical Matchbox play scene—this time a Hatra Tractor Shovel (No. 69) loads a DAF Truck (No. 58) with more girders. Matchbox introduced two DAF trucks in 1968: the girder-hauling model pictured here and a covered container truck (No. 47).

63

Matchbox's GMC Tipper Truck (No. 26) not only featured a tipping bed but also a tilting cab. In an unusual move, Matchbox articulated the chassis's frame rails separately, as is seen in this photo by the shadow cast under the truck.

undisturbed soil, digging pits, and moving dirt. We made the whirring and grinding noises as cranes lifted their loads and dump trucks tipped their beds skyward. We picked the little trucks up to see exactly how the functioning parts moved—extending cranes, spinning the cement mixer's tub, and running the bulldozer treads along our hands. The play value was great, and perhaps this is why more construction vehicles were made than any other type of small die-cast toy.

In the early part of the decade, the British manufacturers made replicas of their own dump trucks. Models of Euclids, Bedfords, Guy Warriors, Fodens, and Scammells were common. And even though these names

were unfamiliar to American children, it didn't seem to matter. American cars had instantly recognizable styles, but trucks were more generic, so children accepted these foreign makes as stand-ins. It wasn't until 1966 that Matchbox introduced an American dump truck, a Dodge (No. 48). Two years later Matchbox introduced a heavy-duty Mack version, a particularly fine model with a full die-cast chassis riding on large wheels wearing separate knobby-treaded tires.

Bulldozers were modeled extensively and were necessary for smoothing out those little dirt roads in our construction sites. Matchbox offered three Caterpillar bulldozers in the first half of the decade, each one growing

Matchbox produced its heavy-duty Mack Dump Truck (No. 28) with a rugged die-cast metal body, bed, and chassis, then added oversized wheels with knobby-treaded tires. These special tires were only used on one other model: the Hatra Tractor Shovel (No. 69). Close inspection reveals that the words "Lesney" and "England" are molded into the sidewalls.

slightly in size but retaining the same open-cab style. The last Caterpillar was replaced in 1969 by a more modern-looking closed-cab Case bulldozer. This category also includes any treaded tractors without blades and those with excavating buckets instead of the traditional bulldozer blade. From 1955 to 1965, Matchbox made three Caterpillar tractors without blades, each one growing slightly in size but retaining the same basic style. Mini Dinky and Impy made treaded-style construction vehicles, but Husky stayed out of this genre entirely.

Surprisingly few cement mixers were made throughout the decade, although most children's collections included one. If it was a Matchbox, it was probably a Foden. A version was sold throughout most of the decade, with 1968 bringing a larger, eight-wheeled model with a more elaborate mixing mechanism. But because Matchbox only offered one cement mixer in any given year, Husky was very successful with its ERF version. It offered a feature that the Matchbox trucks didn't: a swinging metal trough to direct the flow of cement being unloaded. Budgie was the only other major manufacturer to make a cement mixer.

The "tipper" truck was another popular construction vehicle made in miniature. Although not commonly seen on American roads, it was easy enough to figure out how to use these trucks. Sort of a cross between a dump truck and a container truck, their roomy beds worked well for hauling such small objects as pebbles or twigs. They tipped

Husky introduced its ERF Cement Mixer in 1966. Early models featured an unpainted, die-cast chute, as on this example. Husky installed chrome-plated plastic chutes on later versions.

Tipper trucks featured roomy, square-bottomed beds with tall, straight sides—different from the common American dump truck with its tapered sides and upturned rear. Popular with kids because of its hauling abilities, Matchbox's DAF Tipper Container Truck (No. 47) came packaged with a plastic lid to cover the top of the container.

up like a dump truck, but were constructed with squarer corners, giving them more hauling capacity. Matchbox made four tippers throughout the decade. Their 1968 DAF Tipper Container Truck (No. 47) even included a plastic lid to cover the contents of the bed.

Mini Dinky made some of the best heavy construction equipment. They featured a varied assortment of vehicles, from an International Bulldozer and Skid Shovel to a Euclid Dump Truck and a Michigan Scraper that measured over 4 inches in length.

In addition to several farm tractors, pickup trucks, and a Jeep, Matchbox made a few unique models. Among these were four trucks that came complete with removable loads. Two Leyland trucks were introduced in 1966, one carrying pipes (No. 10) and the other a portable building, presumably a contractor's office (No. 60, Site Hut Truck). These were followed by a DAF truck hauling girders and a Mercedes truck carrying sections of scaffolding.

Husky also produced distinctive models, including a Bedford "skip" truck, which featured a metal skip and support armature (Matchbox would make a similar model in the 1990s). The others were called "tower" trucks—pickup trucks with vertically extending towers attached to their beds. In real life, these towers with platforms enabled construction workers to reach the second or third floors of unfinished buildings, change lamppost bulbs, and install overhead signage.

Service Vehicles

Buses, taxis, oil tankers, garbage trucks, delivery trucks, and open-backed interstate

At over 4 inches long, Mini Dinky's Michigan Scraper dwarfed other small die-casts of the period. This earth-moving giant featured a separate pivoting rear section, as well as black rubber tires mounted on yellow plastic hubs.

A late 1960s Matchbox King Size Guy Warrior Car Transporter (No. K8) unloads its cargo: a metallic blue and a mint-green Lincoln Continental (both No. 31), a red Pontiac grand prix (No. 22), and a metallic green Mercury Cougar (No. 62).

haulers are among the many types of vehicles included in the "service" genre. A staple of most manufacturers' product lines, service vehicles were popular with children because their various specific functions made it easy to create new scenes in make-believe worlds.

As with construction equipment, children were rough on service vehicles. After all, they were designed for work. Buses, one of the most popular groups, included city versions as well as long-distance highway types. Matchbox made 10 styles (Nos. 5B, 5C, 5D, 21, 40, 56, 58, 66, 68, and 74) during the 1960s. The London double-decker bus was probably the most recognizable of the period. Matchbox introduced it to the line in 1954 and it remained there until the 1990s, growing slightly in size through the years. Arguably the exemplar of Matchbox vehicles in the 1960s, the London bus was found in most children's collections. How many thousands of American children, unfamiliar

with this style of bus, tried to trace the path of that tiny spiral staircase from the first level to the top deck?

But the bus that became America's favorite wasn't introduced until 1967: the Greyhound. This was a bus that American children could understand—one that, in its real version, came through every town in America. The Matchbox model is painted in the proper silver color and features a raised passenger area a few steps above the driver, a common design of the time. Oddly, Matchbox cut three large square skylights into the roof, an invention of their own design that helped illuminate the interior.

Of the other major manufacturers, only Husky made a bus, the Duple Vista 25. (Mini-Lindy did make a Greyhound bus plastic model kit.) The Husky featured three skylights (of a more reasonable size) in the roof. Having never ridden in a Duple Vista bus, I can only assume that they are a correct detail. Husky's handsome Duple Vista featured a

Matchbox made 10 different buses throughout the 1960s. Only one was American: the Greyhound (No. 66).

Is this the most famous Matchbox vehicle? Even though real double-decker buses were far from common in this country, almost every American child was familiar with them because of this toy. Matchbox issued its first London Bus in 1954. This model (No. 5) debuted in 1965. The classic London bus remained in Matchbox's line through the 1990s—just when most of the real versions seemed to end up in New York City as tour buses.

white upper body (in plastic) and a die-cast lower body painted turquoise. In 1969, the Duple Vista featured the more refined Husky wheel type: a chromed-plastic hub with separate rubber tire.

Taxis, although ideal for working into imaginary scenes, were less commonly reproduced. Matchbox only made two during the decade: the British Austin "black cab" (painted dark red) and a 1964 Chevrolet Impala (one of this author's all-time favorites). Budgie also made the classic Austin taxi, but, inexplicably, other manufacturers stayed away from taxis altogether. The classic American taxi, the Checker Marathon, was never modeled in this scale.

Delivery vans, however, were widely made. These were fun to play with, too, because many had opening doors that allowed miniature cargo to be loaded. One of my favorites is Budgie's R.E.A. Express delivery van, featuring the slogan, "Some carriers still cost less than R-E-A painted

Husky made only one bus, the Duple Vista 25. This gently used example rides on Husky's later wheel type: chromed plastic hubs with separate black plastic tires. The Vista 25 features a die-cast base (painted turquoise) and a white plastic window and roof section with three skylights.

All-metal construction (except for the tires) was the Budgie style. They never introduced interiors and window glazing as regular features on their small-scale vehicles. This delivery truck, although already enjoyed by some child of the 1960s, elicits a smile from adults today because of its clever advertising slogan.

on each side along with the likeness of a carrier pigeon.

Oil tankers, another popular model type, were necessary for "refilling" our imaginary service stations. Matchbox's "Road Tanker" was introduced in 1955; it was replaced by a slightly larger model (of the same truck) in 1958. In 1964 a new model debuted, this time the truck was a Bedford (featuring a flip-over cab to display the engine), which sported the familiar green and yellow colors of British Petroleum. In 1968 a new version of the "BP" tanker was introduced, although Matchbox changed the truck to a Leyland.

Budgie, recognizing early on the ease of creating new models by simply painting existing castings with different colors and liveries, based six vehicles on their "Tanker Truck" casting. Variations included Mobil, Shell, and "BP Racing Service."

The play value inherent in garbage trucks made them popular with kids. Matchbox,

Husky, and Budgie all produced them. In fact, Matchbox offered three versions over the decade, each one growing larger and adding a more sophisticated dumping action. The last one, a Ford (No. 7) introduced in 1966, featured a clever scissors-like mechanism that lifted the rear guard out of the way as the garbage container tilted upwards to dump its contents out the back.

Low-sided, open-backed, heavy-duty highway trucks (usually called "open lorries" by the British makers) are unlike most trucks in the United States. Toy manufacturers made numerous replicas of these large, high-speed trucks designed for hauling goods over long distances. Americans were used to dump trucks and trucks with completely flat beds, not these low-sided "open lorries" of Britain. Even so, they were popular toys because they were easy to load up with whatever needed to be hauled. Matchbox introduced a classic example in 1968: a

Although Husky made a garbage truck with a similar scissors-like dumping action, only Matchbox cast the rear section in metal. This Ford Dumper (No. 7) was introduced in 1966, remaining unchanged until it was fitted with Superfast wheels in 1970.

Mercedes truck, painted turquoise and featuring an orange plastic canopy and a matching trailer. This type of double-trailer truck wasn't even legal in many states at the time, but it was an ideal toy. The trailer's front axle pivoted, as on a child's wagon, and we watched with great pleasure as that axle assembly swung around when the truck made its turns.

Unlike Matchbox, which usually left the truck beds empty, Husky added "fake" loads of coal or sand, which took some of the fun out of playing with them. However, when displayed, these loads can add considerable interest to the vehicles.

A number of specialty trucks were made in the 1960s. Matchbox and Husky pro-

duced several designed to transport animals, usually horses or cattle. A vehicle unique to Matchbox was their "Kennel Truck" (No. 50), introduced in 1969. It was a Ford pickup truck with a transparent plastic camper top, under which stood four (removable) white plastic dogs.

Matchbox made an ice cream truck (No. 47), complete with a man selling cones from the back. They also produced the "Snow Trac" (No. 35), a treaded vehicle designed to travel in heavy snow. Husky produced two unique vehicles of their own: an airport luggage loader and a television camera car. The former was a variation of their Volkswagen pickup truck, but with a tilting conveyor belt attached to the back. The television

Matchbox introduced its Mercedes-Benz Lorry (No. 1) in 1968 with a companion matching trailer (No. 2). This photograph shows a regular wheels version on the right and a Superfast version on the left. Both could be found with orange or yellow plastic canopies.

The two pigs in this photograph are stand-ins for the cattle that went out to pasture years ago. The Matchbox Dodge Cattle Truck (No. 37), introduced in 1966, originally featured a plastic chassis. In today's market those versions command a slightly higher price than later models made with a metal chassis.

camera car used Husky's Studebaker Wagonaire (station wagon) body casting, but replaced the sliding rear roof section with a
pivoting television camera. This model
evokes the era, not only because the car is
from 1964, but because of the period (squar-
ish) shape of the camera itself.

Emergency Vehicles

Police cars, ambulances, wreckers, fire trucks,
and fire chief cars—these are the five most popular types of emergency vehicles. Most manufacturers included at least one of each in their
product line during the 1960s. Even Hot
Wheels cars featured a "Custom Police

One of the most unusual miniature vehicles of the 1960s, Husky's Studebaker Wagonaire carries a television cameraman in the back. He rotates 360 degrees to get the best shot. The rear windows are tinted dark blue to hide the fact that he has no legs.

Penny's Alfa Romeo 2600 Pantera wears olive-green paint, an image of a leaping panther, and the numbers 777 on its right side. Italy used the *pantera* (panther in English) to symbolize the speed and agility of its police force. The numbers 777 are Italy's version of our 911.

Cruiser" (really a 1968 Plymouth Fury with mag-style wheels and red-line tires). More curious, perhaps, are the companies that didn't offer any of these vehicles: Mini Dinky, Cigarbox, Johnny Lightning, and Mercury.

For children, emergency vehicles became some of their favorite toy cars. Make-believe accidents were common, and these vehicles were always ready to help. Working features such as extending ladders on fire engines and functional hooks on tow trucks made playing with these toys particularly engaging.

Police cars were especially fun because they could be used to chase imaginary law-breakers. Strangely, Matchbox waited until 1963 to produce their first police car (a 1961 Ford Fairlane)—10 years after the first Matchbox vehicle was introduced. Although the cars changed, the number 55 slot in the Matchbox lineup remained a police car throughout the decade. It started with the Fairlane in 1963, then in 1966 was replaced by a 1965 Ford Galaxie, and in 1968 a Mercury Park Lane (from the same year) took the spot.

Husky made a Volkswagen Beetle police car and, for the American market, they created a highly unlikely police car from their existing 1959 Buick Electra casting. Real Buick police cars were rare in 1959, but a luxury coupe version made no sense at all.

Impy, Siku, and Schuco all produced police vehicles based on Mercedes-Benz 200 series cars. Siku and Schuco also made Porsche versions. Among others of note are Budgie's Wolseley and Rover police cars, and Penny's Alfa Romeo 2600 Sprint Pantera. Painted authentic light olive green, this die-cast gem sports the Italian police department's leaping panther image and the emergency telephone number "777" on its doors.

Ambulances were also well represented. Matchbox introduced their first in 1956, and offered five different models throughout the 1960s. But unlike their police car, which retained the number 55 through model changes, new ambulance models appeared while old castings were retained in the line. The one exception was No. 14, which began as a Daimler model in 1956, but was replaced by a Bedford in 1962.

In 1965 Matchbox introduced one of their most popular models, the 1964 S&S Cadillac.

Matchbox's only American ambulance of the 1960s, the Cadillac S&S (No. 54) was one of a handful of models that appeared in most children's collections. Introduced in 1965, it remained in the line for three years after the more modern and detailed Mercedes-Benz "Binz" Ambulance (No. 3) appeared in 1968.

Along with the Ferrari Berlinetta and the Rolls-Royce Silver Shadow, the Cadillac ambulance was a staple in most children's collections. In hindsight, it was actually a bit dull compared to the Mercedes-Benz "Binz" ambulance that was introduced in 1968. The "Binz" featured an opening rear door and a removable stretcher complete with injured victim. These two models soldiered on into the Superfast years, with the Cadillac lasting until 1970 and the Mercedes until 1972.

Husky used their Citroën casting to produce both a civilian and army ambulance. In another far-fetched attempt to interest American children, the company painted their existing Studebaker Lark Wagonaire casting white, applied a red cross sticker to the hood, and *Voila!*, an American ambulance with an open-air roof.

Other ambulances of note are Impy's beautifully rendered Volkswagen Microbus, which featured opening side doors and engine cover, and Siku's Mercedes-Benz "Binz," which re-mains a staple of their line (updated through the years) even today.

Wreckers, (or "wreck trucks" as they are called in Great Britain) have been reproduced in Matchbox size since the late 1950s. All types have been made, from pickup truck–based models such as Husky's Ford F350, to heavy-duty versions such as Matchbox's Ford "Heavy Wreck Truck" (No. 71). The best-known tow truck of the decade is probably the green and yellow "BP"-Dodge made by Matchbox (No. 13). It

Introduced in 1965, Matchbox's Dodge Wreck Truck (No. 13) was a hit in the United States because it was the first model of an American wrecker produced by the toy company. In this photograph, a Mini Dinky Jaguar XKE rides on its tow hook.

was introduced in 1965 and made the transition to the Superfast line in 1970, its last year of production. Most had a yellow cab and a green rear section; find one with a green cab and a yellow back and it could fetch over $1,000 at auction.

Fire trucks, sometimes featuring removable or extending rescue ladders, are arguably the most interesting emergency vehicles. A commonly reproduced model was the British "Merryweather Marquis." Matchbox, Budgie, and Fun Ho! all made one. Impy made a beautifully detailed Merryweather fire engine with a rotating and extending ladder. Americans had to wait until 1966 for a fire engine familiar to them: Matchbox's Fire Pumper Truck (No. 29). To make the American connection absolutely clear, many of these pumpers had "Denver" decals applied to each door.

Fire chief cars are the scarcest of all emergency vehicles. Throughout the decade,

Matchbox made only two: a 1961 Ford Fairlane and a 1965 Ford Galaxie. The body castings were "borrowed" from their police car counterparts, which Matchbox issued simultaneously.

Like their Buick Electra police car, Husky used an existing casting—the Jaguar Mark X—to create their only fire chief car. (The company actually made two Jaguar Mark X fire chief cars, the second one growing slightly in size and featuring a metal base plate instead of chrome-plated plastic.) This was quite a stretch since the idea of fire chief cars in general is a foreign notion in Britain. A luxury Jaguar version is even more preposterous.

More-believable fire chief cars came from Impy, which used its Ford Corsair casting, and Budgie, with its Rover 105R and Wolseley 6/80. All three of these cars were four-door versions of common sedans—just the type used for real-life fire and police cars.

Husky, shameless in creating emergency vehicles from existing civilian-automobile castings, made this fire chief car by cutting a hole in the roof of its Jaguar Mark X, installing a chromed-plastic siren, and painting the body red. The idea of the fire chief car was relatively unknown in the United Kingdom; a luxury sedan version was even more unlikely.

CHAPTER №7

ALL IN THE FAMILY:
Sedans, Station Wagons, and Trailers

Family Cars

When most people think of toy cars they usually imagine miniature versions of the real vehicles they see every day. These include family cars such as station wagons and sedans, everyday two-door coupes, and even convertibles. Ironically, versions of these American cars were rarely made in Matchbox size in the 1960s.

The only American four-door sedan made by Matchbox during this period was a 1964 Chevrolet Impala, and it was only sold as a taxi. Budgie did make an accurate but simple model of an Oldsmobile Town Sedan. Not a single American four-door sedan was made by Husky, Hot Wheels cars, Mini Dinky, Impy, or Majorette.

British four-door sedans, however, were modeled extensively. Matchbox made 12 during the decade, as well as one French car (No. 66 Citroën DS) and one Italian car (No. 56 Fiat 1500). Unfortunately for American kids, most of these foreign sedans were unfamiliar since their full-size counterparts were rarely imported to the United States.

There's no mistaking that the upright, formal grill pictured here belongs to a Mercedes-Benz. This model, a 300SE, was introduced by Matchbox in 1968 (No. 46) and was one of a very few Matchbox cars to feature both an opening trunk and opening doors.

Siku's imposing Oldsmobile Ninety-Eight seems proportionately flatter and longer than the actual car, perhaps taking styling cues from the illustrations found in car advertisements of the era. This model features an opening trunk complete with spare tire.

Two-door family cars fared much better. Although they weren't always American cars, their real-life counterparts were seen in this country. The Volkswagen Beetle was made by Budgie, Husky, Siku, Cigarbox (Speedline), Hot Wheels cars (custom version), and Matchbox (rally version). Matchbox also made a Volkswagen 1600TL fastback, a Pontiac Grand Prix, and a Chevrolet Impala (1959 model). Notable too are Husky's 1965 Oldsmobile Starfire Coupe, Mini Dinky's early Chevrolet Chevy II, and Cigarbox's 1967 Ford Galaxie XL-500.

American station wagons were occasionally reproduced in miniature. Matchbox made three American wagons in the 1960s: a Ford Fairlane (actually, a 1959 model), a 1965 Studebaker Lark Wagonaire, and a 1968 Mercury Commuter. The Wagonaire featured a retractable rear roof section, just like on the real car, and the Commuter came with two plastic dogs sitting in the back, looking over the tailgate.

Convertibles were fairly scarce, considering how popular they were in America during the 1960s. Budgie made a Plymouth Belvedere (actually a late 1950s

Majorette often packaged its miniature Citroën DS 21 with a boat or camping trailer. This French-made model of a classic French car features an opening hood and trunk, as well as a full interior, window glazing, plastic headlight covers, and working suspension.

Two features mark this Peugeot 404 as an Impy Flyer: the teal color and the absence of rhinestone headlights. Impy painted the original versions metallic blue or light green, and like all Impy cars made before 1968, used real glass headlights.

model), Matchbox made a 1960 Pontiac Bonneville (introduced in 1962), and Siku made sensational models of a 1965 Pontiac Bonneville and a 1965 Pontiac GTO.

Trailers

Designed to be pulled behind a miniature car, die-cast trailers of the 1960s came in three basic styles—camping, boat, and horse—as well as a few specialized models such as Matchbox's motorcycle trailer and its Mobile Refreshment Canteen. Trailers were a common addition to many die-cast toy lines in the 1960s, with Matchbox, Husky, Siku, Majorette, Tootsietoy, Penny, and Fun Ho! each featuring at least one. Matchbox offered the greatest variety (Ten in all), and Siku and Majorette often packaged trailers and cars together. But some manufacturers—Mini Dinky, Impy, Budgie, Cigarbox, Johnny Lightning, Mercury, Schuco, and Mattel's Hot Wheels cars—produced no trailers.

Almost a "modern" Matchbox car, this Pontiac Bonneville Convertible (No. 39) features a plastic interior and windshield but is not yet fitted with working suspension. The Bonneville model was introduced in 1962, but the photograph shows a toy from 1966. Earlier models rode on silver or gray plastic wheels, not black.

Majorette produced its dual Kayak trailer from the 1960s until the 1990s. The boats are held in place with tension created by the upper mounting arms and the tops of each fender.

Matchbox included a camping trailer in its line throughout the 1960s. The Bluebird Dauphine (No. 23) appeared in 1960, but it wasn't until 1965 (with the No. 23 Trailer Caravan) that an interior was replicated, making it easy to imagine sitting down at the miniature dining table, or stepping out onto the open-air porch at the rear. The white plastic roof lifted off to better see the layout inside.

Speedboats were also very popular. Matchbox offered three over the decade. Husky, Siku, Penny, and Tootsietoy each made their own, and Majorette even offered a trailer that held two kayaks. The actual trailers were die-cast metal, but the boats themselves were made of hollow plastic so that they could float. Husky, riding on parent company Corgi's licensing success with the James Bond Aston Martin, holds the distinction of producing the Batboat (1968), designed to be pulled behind its Batmobile (1967).

Horse trailers, also a favorite, were made by Matchbox, Husky, and Majorette. These all included plastic horses and featured hinged gates in the back that dropped to the ground for loading and unloading.

Matchbox offered several unique models. In 1967 it introduced the Honda Motorcycle

Husky issued its Sports Boat in 1969, the last year before changing the brand's name to Corgi Junior. Only models produced in that year featured the word Husky molded into the boat's hull.

One of Husky's later models, the Rice Beaufort Horse Trailer was introduced in 1968 with the handsome chromed-hub wheel type. Early Corgi Junior models, beginning in 1970, were identical except for paint color.

& Trailer (No. 38). This model included a finely cast motorcycle featuring wire wheels and separate black plastic tires that slipped snugly into wells in the floor of the yellow- or orange-painted trailer. The Honda Motorcycle & Trailer survived the Superfast transition and was finally retired in 1972.

From 1959 to 1965 Matchbox produced the Mobile Refreshment Canteen (No. 74).

Matchbox produced its Honda Motorcycle & Trailer (No. 38) from 1967 until 1972. The cycle itself featured a die-cast body, finely cast wire wheels, and a functioning kick-stand. Its tires fit snugly into two wells molded in the floor of the die-cast trailer.

This amusing little trailer offered, according to the decal applied to its side, a decidedly British menu of "coffee, tea, snacks, minerals, sandwiches, and hot pies."

Throughout the 1960s, Tootsietoy offered a tiny orange U-Haul open trailer, just perfect for carrying a pinch of sand or a small pebble. Fun Ho! of New Zealand offered a similar generic utility trailer, painted green.

Tootsietoy sold this HO-scale 1960 Rambler and U-Haul trailer as a pair. Other models in the "Pocket" series included a Ford Sunliner Convertible, a Ford Dump Truck, and a school bus.

CHAPTER №8

1960S REVIVAL:
New Toys and Collectibles

In the late 1990s a trend emerged where more manufacturers started producing models of 1960s cars. Often, these were cars that were never made in 1/64th-scale diecast during their day. Also, the quality of these new toys and collectibles often surpassed that of models made in the 1960s.

As a result of manufacturing shifts to such countries as China, where labor is cheap, details that were too expensive to include then are now common. Separate rearview mirrors, complete miniature engines, and wheels specific to individual cars are featured on vehicles in the Racing Champions Mint line. Painting technology, in particular tampo (a process by which details can be pad-printed on uneven surfaces), has imbued models with a level of realism not possible 30 years ago. Headlights, grills, even chrome window molding is often highlighted on relatively inexpensive models such as the Johnny Lightning Muscle Cars USA series.

This trend toward producing more models of cars from the 1960s can be attributed to three major forces. First, the directors, designers, and marketing staff employed by today's toy companies are often children of the

Racing Champions made a name for itself in the early 1990s by producing models of vintage and contemporary NASCAR racers. The 5 Decades of Petty series, introduced in 1999, includes a 1960 Plymouth, a 1964 Plymouth, a 1969 Ford (front row), a 1962 Plymouth, and a 1963 Plymouth (back row).

1960s, harboring nostalgic memories of the cars from that era. Second, a renaissance in the popularity of real muscle cars began in the early 1990s. Car collectors started to take these factory hot rods more seriously when pristine examples started fetching prices above $50,000 at auction.

Third, the NASCAR licensing frenzy of the 1990s not only brought the sport to a wider audience, but in many of its new fans it stirred an interest in the history of stock-car racing. Books were published that chronicled the stories of racing legends such as LeeRoy Yarbrough, Fred Lorenzen, and "Fireball" Roberts. Old black-and-white photographs gave us a glimpse into the dirt-track race circuit, which featured cars sponsored by local garages.

In the early 1990s, Racing Collectibles (Action Performance) and Racing Champions began producing 1/64th-scale models of early 1960s stock cars. Surprisingly, stock cars from the 1960s had never before been modeled in small scale, and now we had entire fleets of 1963, 1964, and 1965 Ford Galaxies, 1962 Pontiac Catalinas, and 1963 Chevrolet Impalas. These cars were joined by late-decade racers such as 1969 Ford Torino Talledegas, 1967 Ford Fairlanes, and 1969 Dodge Daytonas (the latter two produced by Johnny Lightning.)

Racing Collectibles produced this 1964 Dodge Polara Super-Stock in the mid-1990s. Although priced at about $10 each, Racing Collectibles vehicles offer rubber tires, accurate body castings, and some of the finest paint finishes available on any collectible vehicles made today. In their vintage stock car series, look for the 1962 Pontiac Catalina, 1963 Chevrolet Impala, 1963 Ford Galaxie, and 1965 Ford Galaxie.

With muscle cars and stock cars leading the way, manufacturers today are more confident about reviving other types of vehicles. Siku of Germany gives us a staple of 1960s European automobiles: the Mini Cooper. Hot Wheels cars produces a variety of 1960s vehicles, including a 1963 Ford Thunderbird, a 1965 Ford Mustang Convertible, and a 1965 Chevrolet Impala (albeit in 1990s lowrider guise). The Racing Champions Mint line produces numerous examples, including a 1960 Chevrolet Corvair and Impala, as well as a 1965 Ford pickup truck and a 1966 Chevrolet Nova. And Johnny Lightning's Hollywood on Wheels series includes a 1967 Ford Fairlane four-door sedan (from the *Dragnet* television series) and a 1961 Ford Fairlane police car (from *The Andy Griffith Show*).

These newly manufactured models of 1960s cars are a welcome addition to the toy car market. Before the 1990s, manufacturers concentrated, for the most part, on contemporary vehicles only. If older cars were produced at all they were generally much older, as in Matchbox's Yesteryears series, which featured cars from the first two decades of the twentieth-century. (Hot Wheels cars did produce custom versions of five classic Fords, three from the 1930s.) But today, for the first time, cars from the not-so-distant past are included in the standard lineup of many toy manufacturers. Not only is this a thrill for those of us who remember the real cars, but it is a valuable history lesson for those too young to have seen, for example, an actual winged Dodge Daytona, a muscular Pontiac GTO "Judge," or a quirky Citroën 2CV.

New 1960s vehicles are manufactured both as inexpensive toys and as pricey collectibles. They fall into three distinct price groups: toys, "expensive toys," and adult collectibles. Toys are easy to spot; they sell for about a dollar. They may be viewed as collectible by some adults, but their primary market is children. Expensive toys sell for between $3 and $4 and end up in both the hands of children and adult collectors. Collectibles are produced strictly for the adult market, include more details, and sell for $5 and up.

Toy Cars for Children

Toy models of 1960s cars are primarily made by Hot Wheels cars, Matchbox, Yatming, Siku, and Speed Rebels (a Playing Mantis series). Again, these are all priced around a dollar and are produced primarily for children.

In addition to the current Hot Wheels cars listed earlier, the recent product line has included a 1965 AC Cobra, a 1963 Corvette, a 1967 Camaro, and a 1968 Ford Mustang Fastback (part of their Vintage series).

Matchbox makes a 1969 Camaro SS Convertible and a 1968 Ford Mustang Fastback, as well as a 1969 Pontiac GTO "Judge," a 1963 Corvette Grand Sport, and both stock and racing versions of the 1962 Corvette.

Yatming, a relatively unfamiliar name in die-cast, often calls itself by other brand names in different international markets. Throughout the 1990s, the Woolworth dime-store chain chose Yatming toys as their private-label Matchbox-size die-cast vehicle line (replacing Playart). Cars were individually blister-packed and sold in sets. But the name Yatming never appeared on any packaging; it was usually molded into the base plate of the car itself. In the United States today, Yatming seems to favor the brand name Road Tough, and although not as easy to find as they were a few years ago, they do appear at independent shops and discount stores.

Yatming appears to be existing on castings that were originally created in the 1970s, having only introduced a few new models to their 1/64th-scale assortment in recent years.

Their current lineup includes, among others, a 1964 Chevrolet Impala, a 1966 Ford Galaxie, a 1966 Chevrolet Chevelle SS, and a 1969 Dodge Charger.

Playing Mantis' Speed Rebels were an attempt to break into the true 99¢ die-cast toy market. The Speed Rebels series featured smaller variations of the first round of Muscle Cars USA. They were blister-packed on smaller cards (most other Playing Mantis products are packaged on cards larger than the industry standard) and the first series featured brighter, wilder paint colors aimed at children (windshield glass, for example, was orange!). Four cars from the 1960s were made: a 1965 Pontiac GTO Convertible, 1969 Pontiac GTO Judge, 1969 Oldsmobile 442, and 1969 Mercury Cougar Eliminator.

Expensive Toys

This segment of the die-cast market, best described as "expensive toys," includes most products from Johnny Lightning and the NASCAR lines from Racing Champions, Hot Wheels cars, Hasbro, and others. Cars are priced between $3 and $4. More adults than children buy these vehicles, but they are built for play and surely a good number of them end up in the hands of kids at such special occasions as birthday parties and Christmas.

Since the early 1990s, interest in the whole genre of NASCAR die-cast has increased

Matchbox released this 1969 Chevrolet Camaro SS Convertible in 1998. Accurate proportions, painted racing stripes, tiny Camaro SS script, and Matchbox's handsome five-spoke wheels make this 99¢ model a bargain.

dramatically. In those early days, 1960s stock cars were often modeled; today they are becoming harder to find. Some hope is found with Racing Champions, which, in 1999, introduced a series of Richard Petty stock cars, many dating from the 1960s. In 1998 the company capitalized on the 50th anniversary of NASCAR by reissuing its 1969 Ford Torinos and Mercury Cyclones.

Since its inception in 1994, Johnny Lightning has introduced series upon series of new vehicles. Stock-car toys have been a relatively small portion of their entire product line. Johnny Lightning's growth rate has been impressive, and the realism of their vehicles seems to improve with every new series. Each group of cars is usually made in several color versions, greatly multiplying the number of available examples.

Adult Collectibles

Before the 1990s, the adult collectibles market in 1/64th-scale die-cast was largely untapped. Today these vehicles have become an important part of many manufacturers' marketing plans. Hot Wheels Collectibles, Matchbox Collectibles, Racing Collectibles, and Racing Champions all compete for the attention of the adult collector.

Hot Wheels Collectibles, whose cars often sell for around $10 each, produces beautiful 1/64th-scale models of 1969 muscle cars (Chevrolet Chevelle, Oldsmobile 442, American Motors AMX, and Plymouth GTX), a 1969 Buick Riviera lowrider, a 1963 Cadillac hearse, a 1963 Plymouth (available in the Reggie Jackson set), and many others.

More affordable are models from the Racing Champions Mint line. Priced

Johnny Lightning introduced this 1968 Ford Torino in 1999 as part of their Indy 500 Pace Car Series. Like all Johnny Lightning vehicles, it features a heavy die-cast body and chassis and a degree of realism usually seen in models costing much more. Often priced at under $4, Johnny Lightning vehicles represent one of the best bargains in die-cast today.

around $5, these cars offer unmatched realism for the price, and a wide selection of 1960s cars that is the most complete in the industry. All feature opening hoods, detailed engines, wheels specific to the car, and a generous amount of details highlighted with different paint colors. The Mint line was replaced in 2000 by a similar line called Classified Classics.

Of final note is Tomica of Japan. Tomy (their parent company) sells these beautifully made miniatures as toys in their home market and Great Britain, but does not distribute them in the United States. Tomicas are available from independent sources here but their price ($8 and up) dictates their status as an "adult collectible." Quality remains high, even after recently moving production to China. Most Tomicas are models of Japanese cars, but a few Western vehicles are usually included in their product line. Among them are a Rolls-Royce Phantom VI, a Mini Cooper, and a Citroën 2CV.

Hot Wheels Collectibles produced this 1969 American Motors AMX for the adult market. At $10 a pop, these models are expensive, but all feature crisp, accurate body castings and more painted details than found on regular Hot Wheels cars. Note the body-colored bumpers on this AMX, an option on the real car.

Racing Champions includes this trio of Chevrolets in its Mint line. From left to right, a 1960 Impala, a 1960 Corvair, and a 1964 Impala. Although priced at around $5 each, Racing Champions Mint vehicles provide features usually found on larger-scale models. Opening hoods, detailed engines, and wheels specific to each car are common.

Once a Child, Always A Child

When we were young, we took our cars for granted. We couldn't have known then how much they would change by the end of the 1960s. The benchmark for toy car makers had been the realism found in Matchbox vehicles. Other manufacturers tried to copy or better what Matchbox did—that is, until 1968, when Hot Wheels cars changed the agenda to speed. Toy cars became something different after that. Wheels grew larger and more stylized, paint schemes more garish. Simultaneously, production moved to the Far East and quality often suffered.

Compared to their larger cousins, including Corgi and Dinky, the toy cars featured in this book provide a more affordable entrée into the collecting world. Many of these vehicles can be found for

under $30; Corgi Toys can easily cost three times that price.

Just as children choose their toys simply by what they like, so should the collector. Don't buy only what you think will be valuable in the future. Do buy the best examples you can afford but don't try to collect too much. Take the cars out of their packages and display as many as you can. And finally, be proud of your collection, for it's a reflection of your passion and sense of good design.

Today we recognize the integrity of 1960s die-cast as accurate scale models. We also understand their importance as a record, in miniature, of an exciting decade of automobile production. They provide a satisfying way for adults to recapture their childhood memories and own a piece of the last great era of automotive design.

APPENDIX Nº 1

PRICE GUIDE

PAGE	BRAND	MODEL	MODEL NO.	COLOR	VALUE*
Titlepage	Husky	Volkswagen 1300	20-B	blue	$40
Frontis	Husky	Willys Jeep	5B	metallic green	25
7	Husky	Commer "Walk Thru" Van	19A	light green	25
8	Penny	Alfa Romeo 2600	25	metallic blue	30
9	Matchbox	Commer Milk Float	21	light green	30
12	Matchbox	Trailer Caravan	23	pink	25
14	Matchbox	Opel Diplomat	36	metallic gold	25
16	Matchbox	Chevrolet Impala Taxi	20	yellow	35
17	Impy Flyer	Rolls-Royce Silver Cloud Convertible	22	metallic red	30
18	Husky	Buick Electra	7A	red-orange	35
20	Matchbox	Ford Galaxie Police	55	white	40
21	Matchbox	Jaguar XKE	32	metallic orange	50
21	Matchbox	Volkswagen Camper	34	metallic silver	40
22	Hot Wheels	Indy Eagle	6263e	green Spectraflame	30
23	Matchbox	Fire Pumper Truck	29	red	35
23	Matchbox	Lamborghini Marzal	20	metallic red	15
25	Husky	Oldsmobile Starfire Coupe	31	metallic blue	30
26	Husky	Bedford TK 7-Ton Lorry	27	orange and silver	25
27	Budgie	GMC Box Van	56	light blue	25
28-29	Hot Wheels	Shelby Turbine	6265b	blue Spectraflame	25
30	Hot Wheels	Cadillac Eldorado	6218c	brown Spectraflame	80
32-33	Matchbox	Rolls-Royce Silver Shadow Convertible	69	metallic blue	20
34	Mini Dinky	Oldsmobile Toronado	22	metallic blue	40
34	Impy	Merryweather Fire Engine	30	red	35
35	Impy	Chrysler Imperial	12	metallic blue	30
35	Impy	Chrysler Imperial Police	16	white	30
35	Impy Flyer	Chrysler Imperial Police	16	white	30
36	Siku	Ford F-500	V222	dark green	50
37	Majorette	Formula 3 race car		blue	20
38	Tootsietoy	Earth Scraper		light green	10
39	Cigarbox Speedline	Ford Galaxie XL-500	6107	pink chrome	20
40	Penny	Maserati 3500GT	29	metallic silver	40
41	Schuco	Büssing Open Truck	901	red and gray	30
41, 68	Matchbox	Pontiac Grand Prix	22	orange-red	50
41	Fun Ho!	Car (utility) Trailer	38	green	20
43, 68	Matchbox	Lincoln Continental	31	metallic blue	50
43, 68	Matchbox	Lincoln Continental	31	turquoise	25
44	Matchbox	Rolls-Royce Silver Shadow	24	metallic red	30
45	Matchbox	Jaguar Mark X	28	metallic bronze	25
45	Mini Dinky	Cadillac Coupe de Ville	20	metallic silver	40
46, 68	Matchbox	Mercury Cougar	62	metallic green	25
47	Matchbox	Iso Grifo	14	metallic blue	30
47	Husky Ford	Thunderbird	8B	yellow	30
48	Impy	Fiat 2300S	21	light green	25
48	Cigarbox	Buick Riviera	6109	red	40
49	Matchbox	Ford GT	41	white	30
49	Matchbox	Ford GT (Superfast)	41	white	20

92

PAGE	BRAND	MODEL	MODEL NO.	COLOR	VALUE*
50-51	Impy	Jaguar Mark X	10	metallic bronze	30
52-53	Penny	Ferrari F1	4	red	20
54	Marx Toys	Chevrolet Camaro		metallic blue	25
54	Matchbox	Ferrari Berlinetta	75	metallic green	35
55, 76	Mini Dinky	Jaguar XKE	11	red	40
55	Impy Flyer	Chevrolet Corvette	11	metallic teal	30
56	Husky	James Bond Aston Martin	1201	metallic silver	110
57	Tootsietoy	Indianapolis-style racer		green	10
58	Matchbox	Lotus Racer	19	green	25
59	Matchbox	Volkswagen 1500	15	off-white	60
60	Hot Wheels	Ford Mark IV	6257o	dark red	35
62-63	Matchbox	Hatra Tractor Shovel	69	yellow	30
62-63	Matchbox	DAF Girder Truck	58	beige	20
64	Matchbox	GMC Tipper Truck	26	red, silver, and green	20
65	Matchbox	Heavy Duty Mack Dump Truck	28	orange	30
66	Husky	ERF Cement Mixer	29	yellow and red	30
66	Matchbox	DAF Tipper Container Truck	47	silver and yellow	20
67	Mini Dinky	Michigan Scraper	98	yellow	25
68	Matchbox	Guy Warrior Car Transporter (King Size)	K8	yellow	75
69	Matchbox	Greyhound Bus	66	metallic silver	30
70	Matchbox	London Bus	5	red	35
70	Husky	Duple Vista 25	7B	turquoise and white	25
71	Budgie	Delivery Truck	57	green and white	25
72	Matchbox	Ford Garbage Truck	7	orange and silver	20
73	Matchbox	Mercedes-Benz Lorry	1	turquoise	20
73	Matchbox	Mercedes-Benz Lorry (Superfast)	1	metallic gold	20
73	Matchbox	Dodge Cattle Truck	37	yellow and gray	20
74	Husky	Studebaker Wagonaire TV car	15B	yellow	30
75	Penny	Alfa Romeo 2600 Pantera	35	olive green	40
76	Matchbox	Cadillac S&S Ambulance	54	white	35
76	Matchbox	Dodge Wreck Truck	13	yellow and green	25
77	Husky	Jaguar Mark X Fire Chief	48	red	25
78	Matchbox	Mercedes-Benz 300SE	46	metallic blue	25
80	Siku	Oldsmobile Ninety-Eight	V245	metallic green	40
80	Majorette	Citroën DS 21	13	metallic dark gray	35
81	Impy Flyer	Peugeot 404	28	teal	25
81	Matchbox	Pontiac Bonneville Convertible	39	yellow	40
82	Husky	Sports Boat and Trailer	19B	gold, orange, and white	30
82	Majorette	Kayak trailer		blue, orange, and white	15
83	Husky	Rice Beaufort Horse Trailer	38	metallic green	25
83	Matchbox	Honda Motorcycle & Trailer	38	yellow and green	35
83	Tootsietoy	Rambler Station Wagon	2325	green and beige	30
83	Tootsietoy	U-Haul Trailer	2325	orange	15
84-85	Racing Champions	Richard Petty Series vehicles		blue	4
86	Racing Collectibles	Dodge Polara Super-Stock		yellow and black	20
88	Matchbox	1969 Chevrolet Camaro SS Convertible	40	white	1
89	Johnny Lightning	Ford Torino Convertible Pace Car	479	white	4
90	Hot Wheels Collectibles	1969 American Motors AMX		lime green	10
91	Racing Champions	1960 Chevrolet Impala	125	white	7
91	Racing Champions	1960 Chevrolet Corvair	197	white	7
91	Racing Champions	1964 Chevrolet Impala	38	white	10

* Values are based on mint examples without original packaging.

RESOURCES:
Books and Clubs

Books about die-cast toy cars

Force, Dr. Edward. Revised by Bill Manzke. *Corgi Toys: Third Edition with Updated Value Guide & Consolidated Mettoy Era Variations List.* Atglen, PA: Schiffer Publishing, Ltd., 1997. ISBN: 0-7643-0253-1

Force, Dr. Edward. *Dinky Toys: Third Edition with Revised Price Guide.* Atglen, PA: Schiffer Publishing, Ltd., 1996. ISBN: 0-7643-0083-0

Graham, Thomas. *Greenberg's Guide To Aurora Slot Cars.* Waukesha, WI: Greenberg Books, a division of Kalmbach Publishing Co., 1995. ISBN: 0-89778-400-6

Kelly, Douglas R. *The Die Cast Price Guide, Post War: 1946 to Present.* Dubuque, IA: Antique Trader Books, 1997. ISBN: 0-930625-27-7

Mack, Charlie. *The Encyclopedia of Matchbox Toys.* Dubuque, IA: Schiffer Publishing Ltd., 1997. ISBN: 0-7643-0325-2

Manzke, Bill. *The Unauthorized Encyclopedia of Corgi Toys.* Atglen, PA: Schiffer Publishing Ltd., 1997. ISBN: 0-7643-0308-2

Strauss, Michael Thomas. *Tomart's Price Guide To Hot Wheels Collectibles 4th ed.* Dayton, OH: Tomart Publications, 2000. ISBN: 0-914293-43-5

Clubs
Corgi Collector Club
P.O. Box 323
Swansea SA1 1BJ
United Kingdom
Contact: The Secretary

Corgi Collector Club
14 Industrial Road
Pequannock, NJ 07440

Dinky Toy Club of America
P.O. Box 11
Highland, MD 20777
(301) 854-2217
Contact: Jerry Fralick

Hot Wheels Newsletter Club
26 Madera Ave.
San Carlos, CA 94070
(415) 591-6482
Contact: Michael Thomas Strauss

Johnny Lightning Collector Club
P.O. Box 3688
South Bend, IN 46619-3688
(800) 626-8476
www.playingmantis.com

Kiddie Kar Kollectibles
1161 Perry Street
Reading, PA 19604
(610) 375-4780
Contact: Mike Appnel

Matchbox Collectors Club
P.O. Box 977
Newfield, NJ 08344
(609) 697-2800
Contact: Everett Marshall

Matchbox USA
62 Saw Mill Road
Durham, CT 06422
(860) 349-1655
Contact: Charlie Mack